The End Is Our
Beginning

God Is Speaking Now

ACTS 2:17

God said "There is a Lightning Storm Coming to Take Many Souls"

SK Olson

The End Is Our Beginning
Copyright © 2025 by SK Olson

ISBN: 979-8894791753 (hc)
ISBN: 979-8894791739 (sc)
ISBN: 979-8894791746 (e)

Library of Congress Control Number: 2026905365

The Reading Glass Books
1-888-420-3050
www.readingglassbooks.com
fulfillment@readingglassbooks.com

Presidential Letter

THE WHITE HOUSE

WASHINGTON

May 28, 2024

Ms. Sandy Olson
Saint Petersburg, Florida

Dear Ms. Olson,

Thank you for sending such a thoughtful gift. I greatly appreciate the warm generosity you and so many of our fellow Americans have extended to me and my family.

Our country faces many challenges, but this is the time for Americans to set aside our differences, to try to understand one another, and to strive to make the promise of a just, prosperous, and secure Nation a reality for all. If we look ahead in our uniquely American way and set our sights on the Nation we know we can be, we will meet this moment.

Thank you again for your gift. I look forward to writing the next great chapter in the American story with you.

Sincerely,

My Feelings About President Biden's Letter

I feel this should be said, as President Joe Biden gave all of himself to this Country. He came from a time like myself when World War Two overshadowed everything. The World pulled together in many ways to stop the Hatred of Hitler. We banded together to protect the Jewish people and their right to live their lives. President Biden knew that his Country always stood behind the Israeli People regardless of party. So, when Israel was attacked, nothing was going to stop President Biden from helping them in every way that he could no matter how it would appear to the World.

We all have a right to defend ourselves, but Netanyahu is an evil monster. My heart goes out to the Israeli people. The Palestinian People who are presently caught now in-between Hamas and Israel are being destroyed. The Sixth Trump-et that is leading us to the present End of The World now stands by this Hatred, Lies, Division, and Deception. The Trump-et has come to make way for the one who will bring about the end.

Every heart will be judged for its callous wickedness and its lack of Love, Truth, and Unity. There truly is a judgment, so I hope you all make it. I do not doubt the power of this Universe or its Creator. God Bless you all even if you do not believe.

Table of Contents

Dedication to My Family:

In my family tree, the seed is our DNA, and the roots are all our ancestors that dug deep into the earth having left a piece of who they were. My Great-Great -Uncle Hearne who died in the Civil War fighting for the unity & freedom of our country. My Uncle Thomas Henry 32nd degree Mason, and my Uncle James Henry 33rd degree honorary Mason, were men with kind hearts and great character. My Great-Grandmother Julia A'Hearne Henry born in Fall River Mass. USA, was a woman who let no one pass her door hungry during the great depression. My Great- Grandfather Thomas Henry who came from England, was a Blacksmith. My Grandmother Ethel Henry Russell was born in 1901 in Taunton, Mass. USA, a graduate of Boston University when very few women were allowed such an honor. My Grandfather Russell, who was a Marine, became an operative in WWI and there were many more loving souls that were a part of my roots. The trunk of the tree grew strong with my mother an Eastern Star of the Masonic order, a graduate of Larson College, and attended Yale Art School, she was a kind and bright soul upon this earth, and my Father William Olson who served proudly in the United States Airforce. I myself became a Rainbow girl for the Masonic order, worked on a high-reliability NASA man-rated space program for Honeywell & also ran the Automated Optical Inspection Computer for inspecting circuitry layers for the rocket's Main Ignition Booster on the same program with General Components, we all added something. The branches grew strong with my daughter Candy's husband Gary and their children. My daughter has always been an important part of my life. Steven my grandson was always by my side. David my grandson was always there for me to help in any way needed along with his wife Iyman and my Great Grandson Maximus. Crystal my granddaughter was always with me helping me in every way that she could. Crystal even helped make the original design for the book "God's Visit." book cover which is also now a part of this book "The End Is Our Beginning." Crystal has always been by my side and she has always filled my heart with her kindness, bringing joy into every day of my life since she was born. My youngest Granddaughter Kaitlyn, her husband Louis, my Great-granddaughter Alison and Great-grandson Louis have added to my life in many wonderful ways. Like any tree it was also filled with family that were brought into the branches not of DNA, but of love. They are all a part of my heart and I love them dearly. Our leaves come and go with our successes and failures, but we bloom with accomplishments leaving our fruits for all to enjoy.

INTRODUCTION

This story "The End Is Our Beginning" is a revelation for these times, whoever has faith in any Religion or has a belief that our world is Now coming to a Time of Great Conclusion & Division, we the people need to realize what is happening. The energies on this planet are Divided for a Great purpose. I see it Not so much as an End for many but as a beautiful beginning. All those that can't recognize what is happening they will be left behind in this sad world of Hatred, only about Self, Greed, Lies, and Deception. These are all Satanist Qualities. Those that are of a different energy, on the side of Love, Goodness, Selflessness, caring about all life on this Planet, those that reach out to take someone's hand in times of adversity rather than thinking only of themselves, those that embrace Truth & Honesty, those are "One" with the true Creator of all things. For He is ALL & yet He has chosen those that were of His chosen likeness, that He Himself has chosen to Embrace which is the side of Righteousness. God has shown me worldly events before they played out in the world step for step, word for word. The last three Visions that I wrote about years ago are starting to play out in our world right now. I'm sure there are other people that have been experiencing these revelations, but with your help, we can spread what I've seen take place in the world that will open the eyes of many people. I am not a prophet or one of any significance and I'm sure that with what I've been experiencing many others have also been experiencing. This is not about religion, but I do feel this is connected directly to the verse Acts 2:17. This book is about everything that deep down inside, our inner self is aware of. All those perhaps they are true subjects or maybe we believe in them just to comfort ourselves. Maybe they are just shadows in the dark that hopefully we can ignore. The thought that monsters exist under our beds just to frighten little children. The thought that there are extraterrestrials that could come at any moment, changing our very existence. Demon's lurking around causing unhappiness and misery. Spirits that have not moved on making us feel uneasy, feeling we need to look back over our shoulder as they are watching. All kinds of religions saying that they are the truth and the only way to redemption. I have personally learned that God is beyond magnificent and at the same time he is someone who will never leave you behind or let you down. People wonder why God lets terrible things happen, and why he allows us to suffer. I can only tell you from my own life experiences that if you reach out to God, he will hear you. We are given this blessing of physical existence to learn. We learn not only through our own experiences but through the experiences of others. We learn through recorded history and then usually we still make the same mistakes. Sometimes we learn through tragedy and suffering things that we might have taken for granted or never would have understood at all. Therefore, these things are necessary to help us to evolve into an existence we now can only dream about. When I pray or just talk to God about things that I need or want in my life, I always know that his will and understanding of what I need is far greater than mine. I now know that anything that I go through, regardless of suffering and even death, if it is God's will for me to understand these things, then it is right. Having said that, I also know God has the power to change anything and to deliver us from anything. My book only serves to validate all these things, so if these subjects frighten you, do not read this book. I have shared my thoughts every day with my Twitter friends, thoughts that come from my heart and soul, so I have placed many of my tweets in the back of this book. This will help you to know the real me and how I feel about many things. Please understand that this book has been written as if you were looking at pictures in a picture album each picture tells its own story. Even if the stories were not written to connect you will learn something important from every story, as I did through living every moment that God has blessed me with.

WHO AM I?

My Dad was stationed at Kirtland Air-force Base in Albuquerque, New Mexico in 1952, where I was born. My Mom who had graduated from Larson College was traveling the country going base to base with him until I was born, then she went back to be with her mother after I was a few months old. One beautiful sunny Albuquerque day my Mom decided to sit with me under a tree, we were well-shaded from the sun. My Mom kept me on a pillow in the bassinet because I was born premature and was very tiny. My little arms were the only thing exposed as they curled around my face & head. She fell asleep & woke up when darkness blotted out the sun above the tree, there was an aircraft just quietly hovering above us, and by the time she got up to investigate this darkness, it was gone. She completely dismissed it and brought me into the house. My little arms looked extremely sun burnt, yet they didn't blister & looked like a healed burn, but it did leave lines throughout my entire life, especially visible when I had a sunburn or tan exposing the difference between the top & underside of my arms.

At three I was molested by the family gardener. Then I was saved from drowning at four years old, died at five, and was brought back to life. At six was taken into a sex ring for child pornography and was being taken out of the state, not ever to return. Then given to a maiden Aunt that felt I needed to be punished for the sexual things that had. happened to me.

Went back with my Mom for a short while, then went to Florida, with my Grandmother who felt at eight years old, I was able to take care of myself. After what felt like a short amount of time, I was back with my Mom by the time I was nine, I helped my Mother care for my two younger brothers, one that was mentally challenged from an accident at birth. I lived close to another Aunt who had men come and go like people at a deli counter. Saw way too much there, was raped, and was hospitalized at 13 yrs. old, then sent to a foster home that needed someone to cook, clean, and help on the farm. I walked to this church and asked the minister to find someone to take me. The minister and his wife took me in, and my life became very grounded, school, church, and pilgrim fellowship, and since my family on the normal side all belonged to the Masonic Order, I even joined the Rainbow Girls. Then I went back home to be with my Mom, went to school, and worked at the Southern New England Telephone Company. Married at 16 years old, and had a child four months before my eighteenth birthday. My husband left me just before I gave birth to our child for another woman, but in his defense, he knew her long before me and his leaving was as it should be. I got into a motorcycle accident with a friend at nineteen and we both should have died. I continued to raise my daughter and then met a man named Joseph who married me and helped me to raise my child. Now I ask you, if I was a clump of clay to be molded, was I softened up enough for molding? I am going to go into more depth with these happenings, but I just wanted you to see the pieces of my life, so that things will be a little bit clearer in the end. Intertwined into this mess were supernatural happenings which continued throughout my life. In my 20s, I received four very unusual religious dreams several years apart from each other. One played out in real life and then I began to have other dreams that would play out word for word, step by step. Then I would see larger events play out all the way up to the evacuation of the Gaza Strip & 9/11. Then came the last three prophetic dreams, an evil presence that now dwells with mankind, people being divided, and then I saw the end happen and there were people who survived. Now if you think that should be more than enough for any lifetime, you need to add an extraterrestrial encounter in 1978. Then in 1969 a co-worker that was in her 60s told me about Jesus coming to her and her little sister around 1912 on the rooftop of an old brick tenement house in New York City, a story she had kept secret, as she didn't feel people would believe her, only her Mother knew the story. Jesus had come down to earth within a cloud to bring the message that the younger sister was going to die in two weeks, Jesus told them he was very sorry, but that she had to come home, and her sister did die in exactly two weeks. Then exactly 100 years later from the time she had seen her cloud, a cloud came to me in

2012, with a simple message for all of us. Her telling me about her cloud and the dreams that I had where God had spoken to me from a cloud helped me to interact with this phenomenon where God had manifested his presence into our world to let me know that he was truly with us. Of course, God writing upon the blue sky having changed the molecular structure of lightning into flowing water did make a lasting impression on me. I have written fictional stories laced with truth, the kind of truth that is so outrageous it could only be considered fiction, but today I feel compelled to write the incredible truth regarding my life. Life has always been stranger than strange and because of that I have always wanted to be deemed as normal as possible, but after you read these truths you will realize my life and I am as far from the so-called norm, as it could possibly be. Many of these subjects will be hard for you to believe. Of course, the sexual abuse won't be hard for you to believe, but I felt I needed to add that side of my life to help people understand that I was just as vulnerable in this world as everyone else and that I didn't have some pure spiritual existence upon this earth. My life was tainted with sin and incredibly sad at times. I will not be putting everything that has happened to me in this book, but just enough for you to see a full picture of my life. Our steps together through my life will include spiritual encounters, an extraterrestrial visit, dreams, premonitions, prophecies, God's presence manifesting into this world, physical matter changing more than once on a molecular level, & of course life itself. I now credit many of these things to Acts 2:17, for I believe it has come upon me and is presently coming upon others and I am now preparing everyone that will listen.

I have thought about putting this book together for some time. Since my life has seemed to have defied logic. As if I was an anomaly, I came into this world to testify to all that I know to be true. It has been a strange kind of journey, as everything that I needed to know in the end had come to me throughout my life in little pieces. The pieces have been like breadcrumbs leading me to a final truth. Of course, I was not wearing a camera throughout my life so it is just my word along with any lie detector test or truth serum that I would subject myself to. Which in the final analysis will only mean that I believe what I am saying to you with all my heart, but you still have the choice to believe or not. Those that have been meant to understand what I now know will believe, but many won't believe and even within myself there is so much more to understand, so no matter where you are at this moment on the belief scale when the time comes you will understand. I feel that those that do believe are already headed in the right direction. However, it's very important for me to impress upon you that there will be others that will have supernatural experiences and say that it's God, but understand God is an incredible being of energy, He has no need to give us free will then come down here and possess our bodies. I am not saying that His Holy force can't come upon us and heal us, but what I'm saying is that you must be very discerning about people who say that they have been taken over by God. I feel that it would be more likely that a demon who has deceived the person into believing that he is God, rather than the true Creator of the Universe needs to do anything like that. I would rather you not even believe me than believe a bunch of nonsense about God. Now I've heard it all, that if you have had a Godly experience people seem to believe that you must have a brain tumor, or you are just mentally imbalanced. I will admit sometimes that those answers might be the case, but I have no brain tumor. As for my sanity, I am strangely more grounded than most and have worked on a high-reliability NASA man-rated space program (SSMEC) Space Shuttle Main Engine Controller Program for Honeywell & General Components, owned my own Subway Franchise, sold lots of real estate as a licensed Realtor, worked thirteen years for a Tooling Division, TRW Geometric Tool, & much more.

If I was being molded to understand certain aspects of life itself this might explain the beginning of my life. One tragedy after another to the point where it almost felt like this was the way life was supposed to be. At first glance, it is a hodgepodge of crazy random experiences, a bunch of stories that do not seem to have a connection. I am hoping at least you will understand what has molded my final thoughts and feelings. I tell you with all my heart mankind is facing something profoundly important, but we are not alone. I'm not going to stretch this book out to equal a certain length, but rather state the facts, then leave it for those that will somehow take these things into their heart and if any of these unusual things should arise in their life, they will smile and remember my words. There is a part of me that wishes all these things had not happened, but then again, every step has brought me closer to where God wants me to be. Plus, I have learned more about myself and others which would have never been possible if my life had been deemed normal. At the end of this book, we will connect all the dots, but I am not going to make you read through my life experiences to get to the most important part of this book, which is God himself. I will start with the things that prepared me for my meeting with God. God Bless us all, keep us safe, and help us to see through those that have come to deceive us.

ALMOST DROWNED

I was four years old and my mom and I were at Gulfport Beach, Florida on the Gulf of Mexico. We were floating in the water in this big inner tube. We had been twirling and playing around in the water. Neither one of us had noticed that the current had carried us out so far that the people on the beach looked like ants. When my mother realized how far we had drifted out she panicked, and I slipped through the tube. I could feel myself going down, down, as I heard bubbles and sounds of what I imagined were fish. As I traveled down the water felt colder, appearing darker, and almost green. I felt like I had traveled down for a long time while my mother was splashing and groping around for me at the surface. Then something seemed to change my direction, and I started to go up. Then suddenly, my hand was being held by my mother's hand and she pulled me back up through the tube as I was choking for air. The lifeguard came and pulled us back to shore. My mother never knew how she had been able to find my hand.

DEATH AT FIVE YEARS OLD

Jumping ahead, I am now this five-year-old with light blonde hair and green eyes, an extremely independent type of child who even walked out of kindergarten when a little girl took my doll away from me. Then proceeded to walk all the way home which was about a mile from the little white chapel schoolhouse in Madison, Connecticut. That winter I came down with pneumonia, and the doctor had me taken to Yale New Haven Hospital in the middle of the night. My family doctor that night drove through a blizzard from Longmeadow, Mass. to be with me. They rolled me into the hospital with an extremely high fever. I was brought into this room and placed on a flat hospital bed that looked like an examining table. People were all around me, but I was now floating above everyone in the room near the ceiling looking down at myself. This person in a white coat said, something to my mother and she fell over my body crying uncontrollably. Then I saw my doctor from Mass. walk in, Dr. Hall and she asked for a needle, it was exceedingly long, silver, and shiny on the outside. She stuck the needle in the thigh of my leg, as I watched from above, I could not understand why the needle did not hurt me. She started pumping my legs like crazy, then suddenly, I was back on the table looking up. I had momentarily crossed over; I had told them everything that I saw happening in the room before I opened my eyes. They all seemed shocked that I could describe each moment that had taken place. There is no doubt in my mind that I had an out-of- body experience.

ETHEL'S, VISIT FROM CHRIST

In 1968, I went to work at the Southern New England Telephone Company on Court Street in New Haven, Connecticut. I was quite young and only got in because I was able to pass their testing. I worked as a long distant toll operator. I was in my teens and after being there for about a year I met this lady in her sixties named Ethel. She was a genuinely nice person who seemed extremely hard-working and down-to-earth. The entire time I knew her she was never one to talk bad about anyone and she never talked in any way that would have made me feel that she had any emotional or psychological problems. I started sharing with her some of the crazy things that had happened in my life, so this one day she decided to share a story about her life. At that time, I did not realize how she was opening a door into my future, that would play out over 40 years from then and it would be 100 years from when it had happened to her. She lived in a tenement house in New York City in the early 1900s. They were brick buildings several stories high with flat roofs, where they went up on top of the roof to hang out their wash. She lived there with her younger sister and her mother. Ethel and her sister dragged the straw basket of laundry as usual, up to the top of the roof. The roof was bordered by a small wall, so you could not just walk to the edge and fall off. When they got to the top of the roof Ethel's sister saw a very white cloud floating by the edge of the roof. She ran over to it because it was so low to the earth and there were no other clouds in this bright blue sky. Ethel ran after her as she did not want her little sister near the edge of the roof. When they both got to the cloud, the cloud opened, and Christ was inside. They stood there just watching as he started to speak to Ethel's younger sister. He said that she was going to have to come home with him in two weeks. I remember Ethel expressing to me that he was very sorry. They both ran down to tell their mother what had just happened. She beat them both for blasphemy and sent them to bed. A few weeks went by and Ethel's sister became extremely ill with a high fever and she died. Her mother was so distraught that she told Ethel that it should have been her and not her younger sister who was so loving. A few weeks went by and Ethel now became extremely sick with a high fever. At one point, it looked like they had lost Ethel. Ethel told me she did cross over, and she could barely see what appeared to be people on the other side of a densely cloudy wall. A man walked through the clouds up to her, she remembered seeing him in her mother's photo album, which was her uncle who had passed away. He put his hand up as if to stop her and said, "Ethel you have to go back." It was at that moment that Ethel opened her eyes and returned to life. Her mother seemed incredibly grateful that Ethel came back. Ethel and I remained friends for the time that I worked there, but we never talked about this subject again.

RELIGIOUS DREAM ONE

I was about twenty-two years old and trying hard like everyone in life to go to work and raise children. I felt at times I was doing my absolute best. I went to bed this one night and dreamt that I woke up and walked through the house. I walked right out the front door and down the stairs. This all felt very real as if it were truly happening. Nothing looked or felt distorted in any way. I turned right to walk down the sidewalk then suddenly, I felt this excruciating pain, in the back of my neck. Something had knocked me down and dragged me down the side of the sidewalk. As I lay on the ground, I could clearly feel the concrete and pebbles on the side of my face. I slowly opened my eyes and saw lightning in the shape of an arm going back into the cloud, I stood up to observe the cloud, it was electrical and iridescent. The cloud began to speak to me. It said, "Sandy, everything will be alright." At that, I felt at peace without any sadness or worry. When I woke up and told people they said, I must have eaten something that night that did not agree with me triggering the dream. Since then I have had Cat Scans, MRIs, and even wires put all over my head to find nothing abnormal. I felt that God was getting my attention to prepare me for something in my future.

GOD, THE POPE, DREAMS
& PREMONITIONS

This is religious dream number two which is the last remaining prophetic dream that took place in my twenties with the presence of God. This event happened in August 1978 the day my grandmother and Pope Paul VI died. The night before these two events took place, I had this dream. I dreamt my husband drove up the hill to our apartment building, but instead of driving to park the car in the backyard, he stopped short of the sidewalk and let me out. When I got out of the car, I walked around the back of the car stepped up onto the lawn, turned, and looked up at the sky. I had never seen a sky like this one, it was gray, white, black, and patches of blue. The clouds were all moving swiftly almost frantically in different directions at different levels in the sky. I could not believe my eyes or take my eyes away from this kaleidoscope of swirling colors. Then someone called my name, it was that same voice that I had heard in a previous dream where God had spoken to me back in my early twenties. I looked to my left and there was this enormous white, iridescent, electrical cloud sitting on the ground. It seemed solid as I could not see the brick building behind it. The cloud spoke to me, but not in English, and yet I understood the words as they went into my mind. It said, *"Sandy, you must go into the house now as there is a lightning storm coming to take many souls."* I did not want to leave the cloud as it made me feel like nothing else in the whole world mattered, all the sadness that I had ever known in my life was completely gone. I did not care about the storm coming, I wanted to stay with this cloud, I did not want to go into the house, not even to save myself from the storm. I felt safe with the cloud and the strange sky seemed almost mesmerizing. Then I woke up, and it was time for work and reality. Everything that now takes place is not a dream. When we came home from work, my husband drove up the hill to our apartment building stopping in the front just short of the sidewalk. I got out of the car and walked around the back of the car stepping up onto the lawn, as my husband had already left to park the car in the back. I turned, looked up at the sky, and was completely blown away to be seeing the same sky that I had seen in my dream. Everything was moving swiftly as if the sky was filled with storms coming from every direction. There it was: gray, black, and white clouds upon patches of bright blue sky, clouds moving in all different directions swirling around fast as if in frantic flight. I was hesitant to look toward the building as in the dream God was there, so I slowly glanced in that direction. I did not see anything, but God had said there was a storm coming to take away many souls. I went into my apartment and clicked on the TV, all over the news was about Pope Paul VI having passed away. I remember saying, *"Well that's one soul,"* but he said many. At that moment, the phone rang in the kitchen and when I answered it, my brother was on the other end saying, *"Sandy, come quickly as Nanny might be dying."* Nanny was my grandmother and she had raised my brother. I went there quickly only to find out that they had already come and taken her to the hospital. My brother was completely distraught and said, *"When I entered her room earlier she said to me, "Donald close the window there is a lightning storm coming,"* he continued to say, *"I told her that there was no storm and that the window was already closed."* He told me that the paramedics did not think she was going to make it and they were right. She had passed away before we got to the hospital. We have touched on two of the four religious dreams that helped prepare me for "The End Is Our Beginning." The greatest love in the universe is God's love for us. It's through that great love that He has allowed us to be a part of the humanity of weaknesses. How else could we have ever understood that true strength comes when we can face our vulnerability?

RELIGIOUS DREAM THREE

Several years went by, and I had another dream. This dream felt so real I sometimes wonder if I was really having a dream or if it was really happening. I was lying on the bed, and it was late at night. I turned to look at my bedroom door, which was open. I saw a black shadow enter the room, and I watched as it walked past the bottom of my bed and along the side where I was laying. Its black shadowy hands touched just above my stomach area, and in an instant, was inside of me. The moment it entered my body I felt enormous fear like I have never known before, the fear was absolutely paralyzing in effect. *I could not move, and I had a feeling that I was no longer in my body. I could not feel where I began and where I ended. I somehow knew this shadow was taking me away from life. I said three times in my mind "You can't have me; I belong to God." On the third time, I felt my body again, and my head fell over facing the side of the bed. I saw a man in a long white robe standing next to me. He raised his arm and passed his hand over the center of my body, and as his hand pulled away the black shadow slowly withdrew from my body and was now standing next to this person in white robes. Then the shadow crossed his arms in front of his face, cringing back and trembling. I watched the shadow disappear right through my bedroom wall. I never looked up at the person who was standing in white robes next to me, but a great feeling of peace came over me and I fell back to sleep.*

RELIGIOUS DREAM FOUR

I felt this next dream would be the last dream where God or Jesus Christ would enter my dreams for an exceedingly long time. This dream was probably the most understandable, in the sense that I had asked a question and the dream provided the answer. Now even though I could reason this dream may have been caused by my own desires and feelings at the time, it sure did a lot for my spiritual closeness and awareness. Before I had gone to sleep this night, I was feeling very forsaken by God. My life had undergone trial after trial, and I verbally refused to believe God could care about me. I felt like I had gone long past the old saying that God will only give you as much as you can handle. Well, I told God that I did not feel he cared about me, and I asked him to tell me if he loved me. There were many times in my life when I asked for a direct answer, but they surely did not come right when I asked. This answer however did come through loud and clear, in this last dream graced with divine presence. When I fell asleep, I found myself in a large velvety green field under a blue sky. In the field was an ancient stone altar. This altar was made of round stones with a large flat smooth surface on the top. There was a stone walkway made of round stones that had been pushed into the ground until they created a smooth walkway that led up to the altar. On my side of the altar was a small stone step with a flat stone across it where one might kneel. I stepped up onto the stone step and laid my body across the middle of the altar looking out into the field with my arms stretched out and the palms of my hands facing up. As I looked out into the green field, in the distance to the left was a man that was dressed in white robes and he appeared to be Christ. He was walking in a straight line across the field. When he reached directly across from me, he stopped, turned then looking straight at me began to speak to me. He said in a calm, soft, loving voice, "Sandy, why have you asked what you already know?" He smiled, turned, and finished walking across the plushest velvety green field I had ever seen. At this point, I woke up with my answer, which was no matter what we go through in life, no matter how much we suffer, no matter how much we can take, or even if we decide to give up, don't ask if God loves you, because he does. It is simple, he does love us. This I shall always believe, and God knew that I felt this way before I even asked. We are not alone in this space of time we call life. Yes, we may be accountable, but never alone.

"GOD'S VISIT"

My husband had passed away on June 1, 2012, at 10:03 am, he had been sick for some time, but he actually passed away from a blood clot. We had been together for 40 years and throughout that time we always had each other's back. When he first passed, I could clearly feel his presence still watching over my Granddaughter and me in the house. After a small amount of time had passed, I started to put some of his clothes in a box, his underwear was a little stained, so I thought I would just throw them out. I felt terribly guilty, as I felt he was watching me. So, when I walked over to the garbage pail, I turned my back to the pail and slowly looked around, and started stuffing these old undies behind me into the pail, as if I was hiding throwing away his clothes instead of washing them. A few nights went by and my Grand-daughter had a vividly clear dream that Gran-pa had visited her. She said he came into her room and told her how well she and Gran-ma had done with his funeral and everything else. He said, *"he couldn't stay any longer that he had to go, but to tell gran-ma to wash my clothes."* When she told me about the clothes, I knew for sure he watched me throw them away and this was his way of letting me know that he had really visited Crystal.

I was in the process of selling my house and a friend asked me to take care of his dog while he went up north for a while, the dog's name was Foxy. I agreed even though I was worried about showing the house with Foxy. It was 2012 in the month of Oct. and I was going to take Foxy for a mid-morning walk. As I left the front outside foyer and walked down the front sidewalk, I seemed to catch a glimpse of a very low cloud in the sky out of the corner of my eye but paid no attention and continued walking the dog. At least fifteen minutes had passed before we came back and as we rounded the sidewalk, I am now taking full notice of this extremely low cloud, about the height of the treetops, framed in-between a large oak &

a fir tree. There were no other clouds in the sky and the sky was a perfectly deep blue color. This must be the same cloud I had seen leaving the house fifteen minutes earlier. So why isn't it moving, why is it so low, why is it the only cloud in the sky? I walked over to it, as I wanted to examine it a little bit closer. Then I remembered the cloud where God had spoken to me in my dreams a couple of times back when I was in my early twenties. I remembered Ethel, the lady I had worked with 40yrs. earlier who then was in her 60s, how she had told me about a cloud in real life that had opened and spoken to her and her sister. From that point to this was 100 years.

I'm still holding onto the leash as Foxy is sniffing the grass and I'm standing there like a little girl slowly sashaying back & forth saying, *"You know cloud, you remind me of a cloud in my dream, the only thing wrong with you cloud is you have No lighting."* At that very moment, lightning burst throughout the cloud like fire as the heart of the cloud glowed red, then stopped abruptly turning back into this beautifully shimmering pearly white cloud. This presence took me by surprise causing me to gasp for a breath of air, and I threw my hand upon my heart saying, *"God, do you hear me?"* as my voice seemed to fluctuate in pitch. At that moment from the lower left side of the cloud which would be my right side as I was looking at the cloud, lightning began to flow very, very slowly with the consistency of water making a perfect letter the size of the cloud upon the sky's deep blue background. Understand electrical energy, changed into the consistency of water then solidified as it wrote upon the sky, just like ink upon a piece of paper. The letter was perfect like something you would see in kindergarten or first grade, so you would know how to write each letter. It was the letter "Y" for yes, I realized instantly the cloud answered yes, I am God, and I can hear you. Now there are those that said to me he might have been saying 'why', my answer to that is God can spell and he was directly answering a Yes or No question. Now I was confused about what I should do next, I thought should I fall on my knees to the ground, as I glanced down there may have been a few anthills, and I reacted logically by not instantly falling to my knees but considering the moment I wish I had fallen to my knees, then I thought, *'what if I say the wrong thing'*. I placed my hand back over my heart and said, *"God, thank you for everything, I love you."* Then Foxy the dog and I quickly went into the house, as I sat on the couch wondering why this had just happened, I couldn't even bring myself to peek out of the window to see if the cloud was still there.

I wish I had it to do over again, as I would have had the courage to ask other questions and I have no doubts God would have interacted answering each one. I had *"Thee"* universal power right in front of me, but it was so overwhelming that I couldn't bring myself to question such a power, realizing at that very moment that I understood the real answer to everything which was, there was no question more important than the fact nothing really mattered except his will, which was beyond question. He wants us to know that he is truly connected to us and he hears us. Let there be no doubt in your heart that this was truly an incredible miracle to behold. Later, in my life in 2017, I started to put all the pieces together. Ethel told me about her cloud which would have been 100 years before mine, as she saw her cloud around 1912 and I saw mine in 2012, then there were the dreams, and premonitions of things to come towards the end of life as we know it. So, make no mistake God the entity of intelligent design hears everything that you say, He knows every intention within your heart. You cannot escape him as He is a part of all creation. He is the universal energy if you can possibly wrap your head around that. He is connected to every molecule that exists, plus all seven billion of us, including all the other universal inhabitants. The realization of many things came upon me that day, even though there had been no long conversation. I realized that religions were a moral compass for mankind and that there was only one God, one Creator for all of them, and all beings in the universe. I realized God knows the spiritual being in all of us, he knew us long before our physical life. I realized He is the God of all of us, even the wicked, and that even though we sometimes make terrible choices, it is all about learning and understanding. In the end, he wants the ones who remain with him to have chosen and understood what is right. More importantly, he wants us to want what he wants, without him imposing his will upon us. It is completely our choice, for he would have it no other way.

Now I want to share something important with you, others have told you this, but I must reiterate its importance. You are incredibly special, and God knows you personally. Do not look to others for approval, people are fickle, even people who know and love you. When Jesus was a young man, he was just considered the son of a carpenter, no one special. When King David was a young man, his father, and brothers thought David was just a shepherd, not one of much significance at that point in time. When I saw my cloud a manifestation of an entity of universal energy, my family said things like, "oh god you're not going to mention that cloud again or Why do you think you're so special, why there are lots of people who believe strongly, you know like those people who jump up and down in church with faith." I love my family and I must say they seem to be a little bit more on board with my experience these days. However, I need no one to validate me or my self-worth or importance, but neither do you. God has a plan, and we are all included if we want to be. Praying is a way to reach out to God or just talk to him as he really hears you. He is somehow connected to all creation; your questions and His messages will come through loud and clear. He will answer you in his time but know he will answer. One time I was upset and crying uncontrollably, I said to him, *"Almighty God please hold me in the palm of your hand."* At that moment, I turned the car radio on, and the song sang, I will hold you in the Palm of my hand. Never underestimate your connection with God or His unconditional love for you. He will use circumstances and other people to help you in life, but if he needs to, know that he is incredibly powerful and does not really need any help to make things better for you.

You have been reading what I would call snapshots of my life and in the end, we will start to put together why all these strange things led me to this relationship with God. We will discuss the prophecies that I have had that have come true and the ones that most likely will come to pass. God came through to me having manifested part of his Holy Spirit into this world and I believe he has come to prepare us. Now it is my belief that I am not the only one receiving these visits nor was that the last visit, so in a sense I am preparing others through this book so that they won't be frightened when he comes to them. So here we go, let us start making sense of what totally doesn't make sense, I could say, *"Why me or why not me,"* but instead I am going to say, *"Why Not You."* That is what this book is all about, it's about "You" and the choices "You" are about to make in this present lifetime. God wants me to share this with You. Just as someone prepared me for what was to come. It is not about me; it is about You!!

Let me say once again, I wish I had fallen to my knees the day God came, then I wish I had been strong enough to stand up and ask Him other questions. I wish I had stayed with Him until He left, but I will take comfort that He knows me better than I know myself. For He loves us all even when we run away. I am giving you the blessing to know not to run away for He loves you!

There is one more strange connection, God came to me in 2012 the year the Mayan calendar had predicted the end of our world. Maybe they knew God would come upon us and they thought that was the end, but instead, it was the Holy Spirit preparing us for what was to come. Even stranger I kept seeing 11:11 before God's visit & they said that was the time the end would occur. This number bothered me so much that long before I wrote about "God's Visit" I had written a fictional novel "Divine Guardian" saying, watch out for 11:11.

Lightning can represent God's wrath, but it can also represent God's Glorious Majesty.
I was witness to his Glorious Majesty.

GOD WILL NOT LET YOUR
ENEMIES DEFEAT YOU

My husband and I had put all our money into our home, and it was around this time when his health started to decline significantly. We finally had our dream home and we had two older grandchildren staying with us. My husband was suffering from a lung disease emphysema and towards the end we had to take out a reverse mortgage to make ends meet. Hospice came to help and to help make my husband a little bit more comfortable with his disease. This one night my husband got up to go to the bathroom and his oxygen cord got caught on the wheelchair and he fell hitting his head on the stone tile in the living room, after having left the family room where the floor wasn't as hard. He called out and I ran downstairs, pushed a button that we had set up for emergencies, then got the oxygen cord untangled putting the oxygen back into his nose. We lived right near the fire department and they arrived in about five minutes. He was transported to the hospital and seemed to be doing well, but we did not realize that a blood clot had broken away from his head injury settling in his lungs. They started to do CPR then when he looked like he was responding they quickly went into a different mode, but then he would start to crash again and they would start the CPR again, this went on for forty-five minutes and the doctor knelt down next to me and said that they couldn't save him, as I was praying at the foot of his bed. They pronounced my husband dead at 10:03 AM, I was totally crushed.

At the hospital, a woman who had been one of his Hospice nurses said to me that since he had died having a preexisting condition, chances were the insurance company would not help me with anything. I did not know what she was even talking about as I was drowning in tears.

The next day I went over to the funeral home to set up the wake and the funeral. I gave them my life insurance policy and they set everything up. A few days went by and the funeral home called me saying that the insurance company would not honor the life insurance policy and I would need to find another way to bury my husband, for those were his wishes not to be cremated. Then that same day the reverse mortgage people said that I would need to leave my home in thirty days because the mortgage was only in my husband's name and I was not 62 years old yet for the reverse mortgage to be legally transferred over into my name. They said I had no rights to my home, even though I along with my husband had put all my money into this house. Then my job replaced me because I was out of work for a week, and since this was commission-type work through calling people, they were unable to keep my space open. I lost my husband of 40 years who was my love, my friend, and the only one I could turn to. I lost the life insurance to be able to bury my husband and to be able to move and survive. I lost my home of a lifetime. I lost my job to make ends meet within two weeks.

After a few days of being totally numb, I went out on the porch and sat down on a chair as I looked up at the sky, I told God that I did not know what to do and that He would have to take care of everything because I was unable to and I was placing everything in His Holy Hands. I told him that my heart was broken, I told Him that I would accept His will. That night I fell asleep while I was still praying for God's mercy. The next day I received a call from the funeral home saying that the life insurance company changed their mind because the doctor who finally put her name on the death certificate stated my husband's death was an accident and not due to his illness. The funeral parlor lady had worked for two different funeral parlors over a period of many years and she said that never did she see an insurance company change their mind once they had refused a policy. Then I received another call this time from the reverse mortgage people. They were giving me a year to sell my house even though I was just turning 60 years old and not the required 62 years old. They said that I could live in my house rent free plus after I pay them off, I would be able to keep all the equity that was in my home. Then I got another job that even paid more money than the one that replaced me. All this happened after losing everything and right after I had asked God, my Creator, to deliver me from this avalanche of trouble that had come upon me.

Each of us at one time or another has been helped, even saved by the angels that God has sent to fight our battles. Do not ever think that God does not have a relationship with you already, for He has been watching over you since before you were born and He loves you.

When you feel like you are standing all alone in this world, just look around you, we all belong to something far greater than this life. You are never truly alone; The LORD God will fight for you; you need only to be still." Exodus 14:14

Even in our darkest moments we are not alone, for he will command his angels concerning you to guard you in all your ways. Psalm 91:11.

BABY BIRD

After my husband's funeral, we all went back to the house. There was a nest of baby blue jays that had hatched. We had all stopped on the front lawn for a moment just talking when one of the baby blue jays flew and landed upon my chest. I was surprised to see this little wild baby blue jay feeling quite at home, then he flew and landed on my husband's grandson and daughter. I told my grandson to put him back in the nest. We were sitting in the backyard and the little blue jay flew to the back-family room where my husband had stayed all the time and he seemed to want desperately to go into the house. He stood at the French door that was glass, chirping at my husband's cat that was on the other side of the glass door. We kept trying to get the baby bird to stay in the nest. When his daughter was leaving, the baby bird flew into her car. They got him out and he perched himself on the top of the car. We put him back in the nest the next morning he lay dead at the back door by the room where my husband had always slept, as an animal had killed him while he was trying to get into the house. There is no doubt in my mind and in the mind of my family that my husband's soul had taken over this little bird on the day of the funeral so that he could be with his family once again.

MY MOTHER'S DEATH

When my mother died, I grieved terribly for almost six months. I would come home and sit at the foot of her bed, as I had done so many times when she had been alive, except now I just sat there and cried until I fell asleep. I remembered when she was alive the moment I would open the apartment door she would softly sing out in this loud voice that seemed to change pitch, *"Hi ..., Sandy"* the same sound she made loud and clear every day. This one night I prayed to God, telling God that I would stop grieving if I just knew she was OK. I fell asleep, but the next morning I was tossing back and forth in my bed just not wanting to open my eyes, then finally I threw myself on my back and flung my eyes open. As clear as day, I heard *"Hi ..., Sandy"* singing through the bedroom. It was my Mom and I realized she was there, she had been so loud I ran through the house asking everyone did you hear that, but they answered, *"Hear what."* So, I went back to the bedroom letting her know how much I missed her. I told her she sounded well and that I would stop crying. Clearly, I could hear the dead, and I had no doubt this was my Mother's soul.

Love never dies, it will stay with your soul forever, it will cross the universe, it will be a part of you floating in & out of dimensional time, and when your soul rests with God all the love that you have ever known will be with you.

CO-WORKER'S FRIEND'S DEATH

Now at some point, we had to touch on this, and I will say many of you will have a problem with the possibilities that were placed in my life regarding this subject. We might as well start off with what you will have the biggest problem believing.

I was working in a company as an inspector on military defense equipment and the woman I worked with had been there for many years. She was nice, but we had never discussed anything that would be considered outlandish or bizarre, but this one day we did. I cannot remember what triggered the conversation, but it was one that would answer many things for me for the rest of my life.

Her name was Eileen, and she was in her sixties and I was in my early fifties. She told me a story that was unbelievable but considering all the things I knew to be true I had no reason not to believe her. She stepped way out of her comfort zone to share this with me, but I also told her some things that were in the crazy realm of our earthly norm.

She was visiting her dearest best friend in the hospital because her friend was dying. She had pulled up the chair to sit next to her friend, placing her hand on the bed. Then her friend passed away, but before she could even move to do anything, she realized that she and her friend were in a different place. The air was thick with gunpowder, her friend was propped up against a tree near the edge of an open field. She was sitting next to her on a tree stump while he was dying from a gunshot wound, but they were not women anymore, they were both men in Yankee uniforms during the Civil War and his friend had just died. As he looked out onto the bloody battlefield of thick smoke noticing the very blue sky above. Then in an instant, she was back in the room as if time had stood still crossing back to this very same moment playing out a couple of hundred years later. I knew with every part of me that she was telling the truth. Then that very same day I received confirmation. There was this young man who worked with us that loved astrology, astronomy, and anything to do with outer space, besides working for our company he was also taking college classes. He came to me that afternoon with an astrology chart, as he had also given Eileen her chart. He smiled at me saying, *"You know I think I'm afraid of Eileen now after doing her chart."* I laughed as I could not imagine why. He said that her chart said that she was an old soul and capable of killing people. I was amazed that these words came out of his mouth. As she had just previously told me she was once a young man in the civil war that had been in a battle killing people. Plus, I knew she would like to shave all the hair off her face, even her eyebrows like so many women drew them on. Another sign that she liked to shave her face like any man would have to do, once again pointing to her previous life as a soldier. I have always known we come into this world from a spiritual world. We are spiritual beings experiencing a physical life. Meaning our bodies are mere containers for our spiritual being. I have always said this and will always believe this, but Eileen's experience has taken that awareness to a far greater level. I now know that when we are born, we come with a physical lineage of the present body along with a spiritual lineage of all the bodies our spiritual being has lived within, along with only a part of our spiritual consciousness so as not to interfere with the present physical being. Example: Christ didn't know about his spiritual existence in heaven until after the holy spirit came upon him when he was baptized, and it was then that he understood about his previous life in heaven. We do not receive that same insight, as this life that we live is an experience that our spiritual consciousness takes back to our full consciousness upon death. We are here to learn and grow through each experience. Now if I have not lost you with all of that, this next step just might do it. Just like Eileen having come back into this world with a friend from a previous life, we sometimes come back to learn what we didn't learn in our previous life or maybe just to finish something and we refer to these people as old souls. I think there was dimensional overlapping when Eileen and her friend experienced the same experience from a different time, as time and space may be layered.

We are energy in a world of matter. Energy, matter, space & time are all aspects of the same thing. Our Creator is intelligent energy & the physical world is a place for us to learn. We are spiritual beings living a physical life.

So, she saw in real time what we call (déjà vu) as the experience was overlapping through her full consciousness in the spiritual realm. So, let us get back to us while we are alive in what we consider the present. Our spiritual being could have previously been born a different gender, different nationality, different religion, different race, or even lived in a different country. So now we are really dealing with all the inherited physical traits of this present physical life but still may have traits from a previous life if they were embedded in our spiritual being. Now that should blow your mind because when I first realized this, it certainly blew mine. Those who are now prejudiced against certain people may have once lived as the very people they now hate. I tell you the thought of this I just LOVE because it is so God-like with irony.

We are all diamonds shining like stars upon the earth, those that fail to shine are diamonds that are buried under mountains of worldly desires. Know that you are more than this life, you were created to be with God for an eternity.

BUSINESS ASSOCIATE'S DEATH

My next story comes from another acquaintance; I had done a lot of business with this man as he was a mortgage broker. We had a meeting set up to go over some contracts, but we met at a restaurant where we lived. We finished the contracts and started talking about some strange things. Our first conversation was about extraterrestrial life, then we moved on to when he had died. He was swimming in the ocean and got caught up in this riptide, it kept pulling him down until he was just drifting underwater. His spiritual being was floating next to his body as he looked at his lifeless self. Then he happened to notice this gray vortex also floating next to him. He had a feeling that maybe he should go into the vortex, but just at that moment someone pulled his body out of the water and they started to do CPR, then he felt as if he was being pulled back into his body, as he was coughing up water and opened his eyes. What I have learned is that maybe depending on how we have lived, we don't all enter back into the spiritual realm in the same way. Some reentries are similar, and some are completely different, depending on the condition of how our full consciousness can handle the experience of our last life. In other words, it would be like coming back from outer space and we needed to undergo a debriefing of our present self or consciousness. The next death helps in understanding this a little bit better.

CAMERON'S DEATH "LATIN KING GANG MEMBER"

I met this man named Cameron who was a friend of some young people, who were friends with one of my older grandchildren. He was in his early thirties and belonged to a gang called the Latin Kings. He told me that he was trying to be a better person because he had done a lot of bad things in his life. He also told me about a time when he had died, and they brought him back to life. He said that he wanted to protect people instead of hurting them because he never wanted to go back to that place where he had gone after he died. He had gotten into a fight and this other guy pulled a knife and stabbed him. His buddy called for an ambulance, but he was bleeding extremely badly. At one point, he crossed over into death and it was darker than dark. He tried putting his hand close to his face in the hope that he could at least see its shadow, but all he saw was black. He was in a place of complete darkness and silence. Not a sound of any kind could be heard. He realized he was no longer in his body, but every few moments, he would feel another soul bump up against him. Then the soul would move on, this one soul that bumped up against him was another gang member he had known back when he was still alive. He wanted so much to call out to him, he kept trying to say his name, but only silence could be heard. Meanwhile, the paramedics were trying to bring him back to life with a defibrillator, and when he finally came back, he was yelling out this gang member's name that had previously died. He told me he never wanted to go back to floating in an eternity of silence and darkness. He said that he would now dedicate himself to helping old people and people who were too weak to defend themselves.

A few years had gone by and I had heard of Cameron defending an old man that was being beaten in a park. This death experience was so very soul-wrenching that he had kept true to his word.

That is why God gave us free will, for it is up to us to want to be with God, all we must do is follow the path that Jesus walked & we will receive help along the way.

If we walk a path of goodness, we will find Jesus walking with us. If we should stray from that path, we will hear Jesus calling our name to help us find our way back.

SAL'S FATHER'S DEATH

Now to the lighter side of death. A co-worker named Sal, at TRW Geometric Tool, had told me when his father had died, he was sitting next to him. He said, he felt his father's soul leave his body to the point that Sal's soul started to rise toward the ceiling with his father's soul, then they parted, and he was in his body looking up at the ceiling. At that moment, he knew his father had died. We are energy, we are vibration, and we are connected to the power of the Universe. We should hold onto this life until the very end, enjoying every moment of God's given miracle, "Life".

MY AUNT'S SPIRIT

My Grandmother was raising my Aunt's child since she was born, and my Aunt passed away several years before my grandmother died. So, I took in my twelve-year-old cousin and I was in my twenties at that time. We all went to the beach; my cousin had met this boy and we brought him with us. It was a beautiful day, a sunny day with a cooling yet warm breeze flowing in off the ocean. My cousin and her friend placed their blanket right next to the boardwalk, while my daughter and I set up our large beach umbrella and blanket a little bit further down toward the water. I was laying on my stomach and every once and a while I would raise my head up to check on everyone. I looked up and saw this woman in red shorts standing directly over my cousin looking down at her. At first, I became very concerned, who does this person think she is looking at my cousin? Then the woman looked up and straight over at me, why it was Aunt Marilyn with her beautiful Aunt Marilyn smile wearing her favorite red shorts. I raised my hand and went to yell out to her, *"Hi, Aunt Marilyn"* when I quickly remembered Aunt Marilyn was my cousin's deceased mother. I slowly started to put my hand down as I momentarily looked down, then I quickly raised my head, and she was gone. I ran up to the boardwalk where I could clearly see in every direction and there was no one that looked anything like Aunt Marilyn. I realized then that she had manifested into our world to check on her daughter and thank me for taking her in to live with me. Clearly, this was seeing the dead.

SPIRIT PLACING HAND UPON MY FACE

Since we have now entered the spiritual side, we have a lot to discuss. I have always been open to the spirit world. I once lived in a basement apartment that was as haunted as anything could possibly be. We had heavy fire doors in the hallway that you could swing open or shut in the event of a fire. Late at night, you could hear footsteps in the hall and then you would hear the fire door start swinging. If you went immediately to look down the hall you would see nothing, but this very cold feeling would settle over your body making all the hair on your body seem to stand up and you would have goosebumps everywhere. Sometimes late at night, someone would call my name. I would wake up out of a deep sleep following the voice thinking a family member was calling me, only to get out into the hallway between the bathroom and the living room to find no one. Then I would go through the apartment to find everyone asleep. Later, in my life, I got married, and for a short while we both stayed, in the same apartment. My husband and I worked at a tooling factory around the corner from our home.

One day I just was not feeling well, and I told my husband that I wanted to go home and lay down. He said, OK and that he would see me later. I went home, but instead of laying down, I turned the TV on. I had watched it for a while when suddenly, I heard the outside door near our apartment lobby area open and I heard someone walking down the stairs. I instantly thought it was my husband checking up on how I was feeling, and I did not want him to think that I just came home to watch TV. So, I shut the TV off and ran to our bedroom by the front door. I heard what I thought was my husband putting the key in the front door and unlocking our several locks. Then I heard him walk in and you could clearly hear his footsteps on the tile floor then he hit the carpet area in the living room. I heard him click on the TV. Then I heard his feet back

34

on the tile coming towards the bedroom, I felt this would be a good time to play that I was sleeping. I heard him stop at the bedroom door, then walk into the bedroom. I felt his weight slowly climbing up beside me, and I could feel the mattress going down. Now I felt his body next to mine then he reached over, placing his hand which seemed exceptionally large, gently on the side of my face. I am thinking that this would be a good time to let him think that he had just woke me up, I threw open my eyes to greet him and nothing was there. I flew out of the bed, with my back up against the wall as I quickly went around the room and exited through the door. I ran to the kitchen to get the broom, then sat in a big lounge chair with the broom stretched across the arms of the chair and prayed that this thing would leave the apartment. This kind of incident or even anything like this did not happen to me again while I lived there. Instead, other things happened, but since those things will take us into two other categories I will mention them later. Clearly, I had felt a spirit, touching me.

SPIRIT LADY, GRAY WALL

My granddaughter also could see spirits, she told me once about this spirit that had attacked her. I believed her, but I was trying not to make a big deal out of it. Then one day I lay down in my bed during the day. Not trying to sleep, but just resting for a few minutes. Out of the corner of my eye, I saw what appeared to be this gray veil ripple past me, like a flowing cloth of energy. Then I sat up on the edge of the bed and there was this dark gray wall in the middle of my room. I stared at it intently trying to figure out what could cast that type of shadow, as there was no light from the outside filtering into the room. I looked away from it for just a moment and it jumped on me throwing me back on the bed, while this fast-blowing wind was blowing straight through my body from head to toe. I could not move feeling paralyzed. When it finally stopped, I jumped off the bed swinging my arms and fists, telling it to go back where it came from in the name of Jesus Christ. I was yelling at it throughout the house as I passed my granddaughter. She said, *"Now do you believe me?"* It continued to visit my granddaughter, but it never came back to me again.

DREAM/REALITY, AMERICAN INDIAN BOY

I was working on the space shuttle program as an A.O.I. computer inspector. Which stands for Automated Optical Inspection. The night before I had an unusual dream; I was standing in the middle of a structure that looked a lot like England's Stonehenge, but in the middle of the circle were circles that had been dug out of the ground making different levels. There were circles within circles. I was standing on the ground level not down in the circles. A young Indian boy walked through the stone gateway and walked up to me. He was small, shirtless with rawhide pants and moccasins. He had coal black hair, dark eyes, tan skin with a slight sunburn appearance, and a bright red bandanna around his forehead with bangs and straight short black hair that came down to his neck. He looked at me and waved his hand across the ground. Instantly the bodies of weather-beaten Indian children appeared, and their little skeleton bodies had been buried in mounds of dirt head to toe, head to toe. He looked straight at me saying, *"Will you help us?"* I was shocked, and he quickly turned and walked through the stone gateway. I followed him through and found myself surrounded by desert. I could see mountains rising in the southwest far in the distance. I asked him, *"Who are you?"* and he stopped and said, *"I am the last of the Comanche."* Then he turned and walked southwest.

Everything now is Not a dream. I went to work but was asked to work in another department as several people were out. When I got to the department, I started working and walked over to the filing cabinet. I noticed a thick book on top of the cabinet. Taking it down I realized it was about Indians. I asked everyone if they minded if I took the book on my lunch break. They said that they had never seen it before. When I took it to lunch upon opening the book was a chapter on the Comanche Indians and it had a picture of how they buried their dead in the desert. Head to toe, head to toe. I put the book back on top of the cabinet. The next day I went to look at the book again and now that everyone would be back to work I could ask whose book it was, but the book was gone and everyone in the department said that they knew nothing about the book. I feel that before I die, I may get a chance to understand what this was about, but for now, it remains a mystery.

PROPHESIES: GAZA STRIP

I dreamt around the beginning of the 21st century that I was walking in the Gaza Strip, I saw this beautiful Synagogue shining not far from me. It shimmered in the sunlight and it had these beautifully colored leaf plants with bright colors planted all around it. It was breathtaking to behold. The closer I came to the building it started to fade in brightness and as I stood close just outside the building, it appeared now to be dull like concrete and the flowers were now dead. I walked into the front entrance that took me to a beautiful garden in the center of the building, but then everything in the garden died and it became overgrown with dead plants. There was a fountain in the center of the garden that was now dry and covered in dead plants. I started to float up towards heaven, as there was no ceiling over the garden and then I woke up. Then in 2005, I heard that Israel was evacuating the Gaza Strip and immediately realized my dream had come true, for the synagogues were now abandoned.

JUST BEFORE 9/11

Before the dream about the Gaza Strip, I kept having this nightmare about these extremely tall skyscrapers falling to the ground. I felt like I was there for but a moment, as if I were watching the people in the skyscraper from above them. I watched them try to get frantically into elevators and at one point I also entered the elevator still watching them from above. I saw the walls close in upon them, then woke up. I thought about why, was I having this crazy nightmare. Not long after those nightmares, the Twin Towers came down.

Sometimes I dream things that play out in my life word for word step by step but understand I have no control over what I will dream or the visions that I will receive. There were dreams that bothered me so much that I wrote them into a fictional novel that I was writing a while back called *"Divine Guardian."*

LOST IN THE WOODS

I was almost six years old and my older brother was staying with us. My mother had left the house having left him in charge. He told me he was going to a friend's house, but he could not take me with him. He left the house, and I was determined to go with him. So, I decided to follow him and when we got to his friend's house, I would just let him know that I was there, and he would have to let me stay with him. I was incredibly careful to stay behind bushes and trees so that he wouldn't see me. We seemed to have gone a long way as we were now heading up a hill and I had absolutely no idea where we were. He did look back a few times, so I had to be careful not to be seen. As we came to the top of the hill there was a big brick house set off to the side of the road with woods all around. My brother went into this house and I waited about a minute before I headed to the door, coming from the side of the house was a big dog and he started to run after me, but I didn't notice he was tied up and could only go so far. I ran around the back of the house and down a steep hill toward the woods. When I got to the edge of the woods, I was frightened again by a man with a wheelbarrow full of chopped wood and an ax. When he saw me, he tried to speak to me, but I was so frightened I just kept running into the woods.

By the time I stopped running, I realized that I was completely lost in the woods. I started to cry as the light from the sun was slowly diminishing, an almost eerie shade of gray surrounded me, and only exceedingly small beams of light were now filtering into the forest. I stopped crying and sat down on a fallen branch.

I started talking to God, *"Dear God, I am lost, and I can't find my way home, please help me to get out of the woods."* I sat there for a moment quietly in case he wanted to help me, and suddenly in the distance I could hear children laughing and playing. I stood up and started to follow their voices. A few times they grew quiet, but then they would start again. To my surprise, their voices led me to a playground behind my school and I now knew exactly where I was as my house was down the street from my school. I looked up at heaven and said, *"Thank you, God, for helping me."* When I got home, I was the happiest little girl as it was turning dark outside and my brother still was not home yet. His friend's mother gave him a ride home in her car later that night. No one ever knew that I had been lost for hours, except God.

When I now look back, I can see that I had a connection with my spiritual side my entire life. It was not something that I had learned as much as it was felt, it just always seemed to be a part of me. What I have always known is God wants everyone to realize that he is with them. All they need to do is realize that and speak to him. It does not have to be some fancy prayer, just something simple. Maybe *"Good morning God, please bless this day,"* or *"Thank you for this day God, I hope things are going well with you."* That is how I have lived my life reaching out to him and now we know he can and will reach back.

CHILDHOOD SEXUAL ABUSE

This opens the floodgates of youthful tragedy and brings forth many questions like how I ever survived all the craziness, and yes depravity of my life. From here on life is presenting what I would consider a phase that I really wish did not happen, but I would not have survived without the love of God.

GRANDMOTHER'S BASEMENT

My grandmother had this old man that kept up the grounds. He lived in the basement of this big old stone house in Longmeadow, Massachusetts. I was not old enough to talk well or make myself clearly understood, but I did understand what was being said around me. My grandmother's Dalmatian Duchess had just had puppies. I could hear them down in the basement from a door in the kitchen and decided to investigate. The door was not completely shut so opening it was not a problem. I was too little to walk down the stairs. I sat down on each stair slowly making my way down to those puppies. When I reached the bottom, I ran into Henry, our gardener, who was very drunk on cheap wine. He asked me if I wanted to see the puppies and I shook my head yes. He had a bed down there and he took the puppies out of the box and he laid them on a dark green wool army blanket. I crawled up onto the bed with the puppies. I played with the puppies for about a minute, and then he started touching me and pulling at my panties. I felt extremely uncomfortable, so I slid off the bed and headed for the stairs. I was trying to crawl up the stairs, which seemed gigantic to me. He was poking my private area, and I started to scream and cry. At that wonderful moment, my grandmother heard me and opened the door. She yelled at me saying, *"What are you doing down there? You get up here right now and stay out of that basement."* I was not old enough to tell her what had happened, but I remember being so happy to see her and my little legs crawled as fast as they could up the stairs. After that, I would always run away when I would see the gardener. That was just the beginning of the sexual path that would unfold. Now I could leave out all this darkness, but somewhere along the way, these terrible happenings built a strong bond between God and me.

SEX TRAFFICKING/CHILD PORNOGRAPHY

After my strange near-death experience and having been lost in the woods we moved to East Haven, Connecticut and I was now six years old going into first grade. East Haven, Connecticut was a small town with a lovely neighborhood. My mother was dating her fourth husband-to-be. My grandmother kept my older brother, and it was just my mother, younger brother, and myself. We had a small house not far from a river that ran into the ocean. There were large homes built along the river and they had large cabin cruisers docked in their backyard. There was a beautiful big stone house behind us built on top of a cliff and several homes below us built along the river canal. Everything seemed perfect on the surface. My mother did not have much time for us, as she did not want to scare away her present prospect for matrimony. So, my brother Billy, who was two, and myself were always being babysat by one person or another. Every day my mother had me put my two-yr. old brother in the carriage and take him for a walk down the street. In doing this I met another little girl around my age, she was probably eight yrs. old. We became friends instantly and she would meet me when I took my brother for a walk. She invited me over to this lady's house for cookies and milk several times we went there. The little girl seemed to know the lady and her husband very well. I thought that they were her relatives, but they were just good friends of her mom and dad. One day the little girl met me and asked me if I could keep a secret. It all sounded so very exciting, so that day she brought me to the house where we usually would get cookies and milk, but this day she brought me to the backyard instead of this small wooden red building about the size of a big shed. There was a padlock on the door, and she said we were waiting for the man that was the husband of the lady that gave us cookies every day. He came from the direction of the large cabin cruiser that he had docked in the backyard. He walked up to us smiling, then he looked down at me and said, *"Can you keep a secret,"* I thought it was strange that the secret involved an adult, but I said, *"Yes"*. Then he told me something awfully bad would happen to anyone who told this secret, so he unlocked the door, and we all went in. I was holding my brother's hand; the walls were filled with pictures of naked people. Men had naked children sitting on them. I was instantly confused but remained very silent. Then he motioned for us all to leave as he padlocked the door behind us. He brought us down to the cabin cruiser on the river and he helped us all get into the boat. He took us down into the cabin area of the boat and it had windows that you could see out of, but the people on the outside could not see in. He told me if I could do what my friend does, he would take me to the toy store and buy me any toy that I wanted. He took down his pants which completely stunned me, and the little girl started touching him and doing other things with her mouth while she rubbed him. As his semen came out, he put it into a clear jar, when he was all done he put the lid on the jar & placed it alongside other jars that had the same stuff in them except the color of the semen in the other jars appeared to have turned a gray color after having been stored. He told me to remove my brother's diaper and to touch him all over. I did exactly what I was told to do step by step, without asking any questions. I was a solid block of fear trying to act unemotional. He told me to put my baby brother's private area in my mouth and wiggle it all around with my tongue, it was like a mouthful of gelatin that tasted like pee. It was so disgusting, and I was so worried that this might affect my brother in some adverse way, and it did. He got so nervous he started to pee in my mouth. I moved away quickly and felt completely gross. We finally left the inside of his boat. As he was putting us back onto the dock, he put my friend on the dock first, and she just left me and ran home. Then he picked up my brother, holding my brother over the water saying, *"if you tell anyone, I will drown your brother."* His eyes appeared as cold and deep as the water that flowed beneath my brother's feet, I glanced at the swift-moving current traveling through the river. I looked back at him completely calm saying that I would never tell anyone, but my body was as cold as ice. I knew he meant to kill us both and I knew the slightest mistake on my part would trigger this disaster. He seemed confident enough that he had gotten his point across. After I had left the boat, I decided to pretend that it never really happened, I thought I would just never go down that way again. I would stay completely away from his street and his house, and I was determined to block everything out of my mind. A few weeks went by, and it was late in the afternoon when my mother announced that our neighbor Al had invited the whole family over to his house.

I was so quiet that evening, my mother's boyfriend thought I did not like him. When we arrived at Al's house, I stayed out by the front steps. I sat there until the darkness of night fell upon me and the night sky filled with stars. By this time, my mother's boyfriend had come out to sit with me on the step. He told me, *"You see that bright star up there? Well, that is not a star. It is an angel who watches over children like you."* I looked at that star, giving it a close examination, because I knew that I really needed an angel watching over me right now. I was really scared of Al, and I was going to need that angel for protection.

We finally left, but the nightmare was far from being over. I just could not seem to make myself feel better. The weekend rolled around, and my mother was getting ready to leave with Bill for another weekend getaway. Then my mother lowered the bomb, "Sandy, I've been meaning to tell you, that nice man Al down the street has offered to watch you and your brother while I'm gone this weekend." I started to cry, rant, and rave, but my mother said that I was acting that way because I was hateful and did not want her to be happy and have a new husband.

She said that I was jealous of her love for Bill and that I better get used to her going away on weekends. I sank into quietness. I was afraid if I told her now about Al that she would think I was just trying to spoil things for her. There was nothing I could do but go through with this wretched weekend.

The dreaded night came, and Al showed up at our door. My mother led him into the living room, thanked him for watching us, and then gave him a six-pack of beer as he sat down on the couch. She was all fluttered to be leaving, that she never even noticed the fear in my eyes as she kissed my unhappy little face goodbye, I stood there, frozen in disbelief that I was in this situation, a frail little girl with blond hair and watery green eyes, standing as still as a statue watching as my mother closed the door. I turned to Al, telling him I needed to put my brother to sleep. He turned his head, looking at me with inquisitive eyes, wondering what I was thinking. Then he said, *"I haven't seen you lately. What have you been up to?"* I lied and said, *"Well, Oh, I've been visiting my grandma."* Then he said, *"Well, I guess that would explain why you haven't come over to visit. Go ahead and put your brother to bed then we can talk some more."* I went in and laid down with Billy, I rubbed my brother's back to help him get to sleep, our bedroom was right off the living room, so I started praying very quietly. *"Dear God, I'm scared, please send me an angel to watch over me and Billy tonight. I will do anything you want, God, just please make Al fall asleep and not wake up until tomorrow. Please, God, please."* The tears rolled down my face and I fell asleep.

The dreaded night cameAl also fell asleep on the couch after drinking that six-pack of beer. God not only answered that prayer, but he made my mother feel uneasy that night about being away and for some unknown reason, she cut her weekend short. By the time we all were waking up, she walked into the house. Al was incredibly surprised to see her, as I am sure it messed up his plans for me, but I was overjoyed to see her. She thanked Al, and he said, *"Anytime,"* then left. It was like this giant foot that had been looming over me ready to step upon me had disappeared. I knew this was not the end, but I needed time to figure out what I was going to do. Whatever it was I knew that I had to do it before next weekend.

The week had not completely passed, and Al was waiting in the woods near my bus stop. When I got off the bus, he walked up to me and, holding my arm, walked me over to his car waiting in the woods. He started talking, saying, *"I wanted to do something nice for you. I thought we would take a ride to New York City and I would take you to the Bronx Zoo."*

I was only six years old, but I knew this was a one-way trip. As we drove down the road, I was trying to think about what I should do. Should I scream, try to jump out of the car? What, what shall I do? If I screamed, he would just hit me, and back in my day adults could hit their children, if I jumped out of the car I will probably die anyway. Then it came to me as we were crossing the last bridge to the interstate and I knew once we got on the highway there would be no turning back. So very calmly I said to Al, *"I would really love to go to the zoo, but my Mom said, to come right home after school as she had plans for tonight, and she will be missing me right away. I know tomorrow she will be coming home very late, and she won't miss me if we go to the zoo tomorrow.*" Then to my surprise, Al said, "*That is really smart thinking on your part. Tomorrow it is. I'll pick you up at the bus stop, and we will go and have lots of fun.*" I could not believe it, he turned the car around, and I was heading home. He dropped me off down the street from my house. He was happy with himself and said, "*See you tomorrow for our big day.*"

I knew tomorrow could not come. Somehow, I had to stop it from coming, but my mother was not home waiting for me, and I needed help. There was a nice Italian lady that lived next to us. Her husband was always gone because he drove a tractor-trailer. I would go over to her house from time to time and she would always make me spaghetti and meatballs, which was my favorite dish. Her meatballs were like baseballs with lots of garlic. I went over and knocked on her door. She was incredibly happy to see me and asked if I was hungry. She was in the process of getting dressed because she had just gotten out of the shower. While she was dressing in her bedroom, I stood by her door and proceeded to tell her the whole story. I was not sure she was listening, but I just kept talking. Every detail poured out of me like water being squeezed out of a sponge. Then she came to her bedroom door and took my hand, and we sat down at her kitchen table. Her name was Anna, and she said, "*Oh my God, Sandy, why haven't you told your mother?*" I said, "*I couldn't, she wouldn't believe me, because she thinks I'm trying to come in between her and her boyfriend.*" Anna said with a firm voice, "*Well, she'll listen to me, and we will call the police tonight. If she doesn't I will.*" I was so grateful to Anna for her strong support. We waited for my mother to come home. When the light came on in my house, we both walked over hand in hand. Anna was determined to make my mother listen. My mother was surprised to see Anna at the door, and my mother was tired and did not really want to let Anna in, but that did not stop Anna. She walked right in and told my mother to sit down and listen. My mother argued that it just could not be true. Al was such a nice man; he had even offered to help her with money.

Anna said, "*Are you listening to yourself? Are you going to believe this man is so nice after what your daughter has told me?*" My mother said, "*But what if it's not true?*"

49

Anna replied, *"Trust me, it is true. No six-year-old could give such a detailed account if it weren't, and if you don't call the police I will."* sister was much

" My mother said, "All right, we will call the police. Then I will get someone in my family to take Sandy away from here until I can move."

I did not go to school the next day, and early in the morning four detectives arrived at our house. You see, there were a lot of children missing from our area. The detective told me that he was going to ask me a lot of questions. He picked me up and placed me on the kitchen table, then he asked questions for a long time. He wanted me to go down the street and bring the little girl back to my house who had originally taken me to Al's house. I saw her playing out in front of her house, and I ran over to her asking her to come to my house. I mentioned that we had police at my house, and she ran away from me. What I did not know at the time was her parents had sold both her and her sister to Al a long time ago in return for the money they used to buy their house. She was around my age and her sister was much older, and they had learned to live with this for an awfully long time. The only reason he had not taken them away was he had permission from their parents for him to take his pictures in return for money. By now Al realized that I was not getting off the bus. I never saw the little girl go to school, even though she should have been going to my school. It was late in the afternoon maybe around 4:00 PM when Al pulled into his driveway. About a minute later, an unmarked police car pulled in behind his car. They jumped out of their cars and told him to place his hands on the hood of the car. The police had search warrants for everything. They found the pornography in the trunk of his car, in the shed, and on his boat. Plus, they found the gray jars with semen just like I had told them. We were watching everything from a side window in our living room. The little girl and her sister were taken into protective custody and given to their grandma. I was sent to live with my great- grandmother and great-aunt until my mother could move. Living with my great-aunt was a different kind of nightmare.

BEING ISOLATED

My great-grandmother and her daughter, my great-aunt, were raising my cousin, who was my aunt's child, and she was six months older than me. My great aunt felt that since I had been through this sex situation, that made me damaged and totally taboo when it came to me interacting with my innocent cousin. They shielded Debby from day one and I was not allowed to speak or play with her. I was given breakfast in the morning and put outside to play. Debby would wave at me from inside her window. My day consisted of walking up and down the street. Sometimes I would stop and play on this lady's front porch. I pretended to have friends and made up my own games. I knew every crack in the sidewalk for one solid block. I would save some of my breakfast in a napkin to feed the squirrels or birds, depending on which one wanted to be my friend that day. I was let in to go to the bathroom, but I was not allowed to doddle. No matter what the weather, this was the program that I needed to follow. If it rained, I would stay on some neighbor's porch. The weather was getting cooler, as we were in New England and an early frost caused the leaves to change color. My cousin was in school, but they had not started me as I was told my mother would be getting me soon. I would collect leaves, and sometimes my lunch would be handed out to me, usually a peanut butter and jelly sandwich. When I came in for dinner I ate and then was sent to bed. I had no toys, but I did have a couple of stuffed animals. My great Aunt said they gave her a shoe to play with when she was little. I became extremely sick from being out in the rain, and I spent three days and nights alone in my room. I was so happy to be outside again when I started to feel better. People on the street began to wonder about me. One lady asked me if I had a home; another lady called me God's child, and this was not the last time I would hear that say about me. One night I was crying, and my great-grandmother told my great-aunt to bring me to her and place me in her lap. My great-grandmother Julia Henry was frail, but my aunt did as she was told. My great- grandmother rocked me for a long time. I will never forget that night. Only a couple of days had passed from that night and my mother came and got me to take me to our new home in New Jersey. I was not away from my mother for a very long time, but it felt like an eternity.

FOSTER HOME NUMBER ONE

The truly horrible part of being a minor is that you have no say and no rights. Everyone controls your life as if you were an object with no thoughts concerning your feelings or desires. If you try to rebel, it will only make things worse. Life can be hell, but when hell starts at an early age it almost becomes a comfortable state of being. We all adapt, but children adapt much faster, and they learn to survive in their surroundings. I could not feel sorry for myself as I was able to recognize misery everywhere. I had been violently raped by a man my family considered a friend, so obviously protective services now felt I could do without the love and support of my family. I had just left the hospital and was being taken home to collect a few clothes before being taken to this unknown home. I was told that my foster mother needed a daughter to help her cook, clean, and do chores around the farmhouse. I collected a few things from my house but felt numb. I looked back and saw my mother standing in the doorway looking so sad as she watched me leave. I did not blame her for anything that had happened. As we drove over to my future home, my thoughts were not fixed on myself, but on a young girl that had shared the hospital room with me. She was about my age and had been sent to a home for girls when she was very little. I understood it to be something like an orphanage. Another girl at her orphanage had stuck a stick in her eye, leaving her with only one eye. When she would try to go to sleep at night, she would bang her head into her pillow for a long time and then would finally drift off to sleep. I will never forget waking up to her throwing ice cream cups at me. I guess it was her way of saying, "Hi" and wanting to be my friend by giving me ice cream.

It did feel rather perplexing at the time since I was dodging and ducking her triggered action of good intentions. There she was thrown into a cruel world from the beginning, with no mother or father or anyone to hold her and say everything will be alright. Living off her instincts of survival. I did get to know her, and I grieve with the thoughts of the loneliness and drowning reality that I knew she was feeling, these thoughts felt like they were crushing my heart. For me at that moment in time, reality only exposed all your limitations, while dreams knew no boundaries. On the other hand, you can face your realities, giving you the power to make your dreams come true. Dreams alone will fade just as each day fades into the night, but it is up to you to never let them die and it is through that act of refusing to give up in spite of all odds, that unyielding determination is what will bring you blessings that you could never imagine. I could not help but ask myself, *"Why does life have to be so complicated?" "Why does life have all these unique games that you don't really want to play?"* At thirteen years old, I thought all men were creatures controlled by their desires. They liked the mystery, a challenge, and at the same time desired life to be basic with meals on the table and sex anywhere. They were afraid of commitment and responsibility as that put a damper on their thrill-seeking and their ability to conquer all challenges laid before them. The only thing that saves a woman is somewhere in all of that there is still a little boy that falls in love with the little girl inside of the woman that he adores. As for women, they do not make sense at all. Women want to be independent and at the same time they usually pick a man that is controlling. They want to be desired like a goddess while wanting a family to fulfill their desire to nurture. All these feelings need to be addressed, but even at thirteen years old I knew our time on the earth was short, and we should make the best of every moment, as far too soon it is all too late. Well, we finally made it to my new home. I was a born and bred city girl, and this was a home with a barn and chickens. It wasn't too bad, but my room at the back of the house was the pits. The room sloped downward, and it had rat holes in the floor by my dresser. There was a single bed, no pictures, no mirror, and only one small window that faced the barn. This was supposed to be my home until I was eighteen. I was determined to make the best of things. I pushed the dresser over a little bit to cover up part of the rat holes. Put my suitcase on the bed and started to unpack. I thought I will just wrap myself up well inside the sheet and blanket, then maybe the rat will not get me.

The people who had taken me in seemed genuinely nice. I was a replacement for their daughter. Her daughter was all grown with a family of her own and Mrs. Thompson needed someone to help her around the place, she was a German woman that loved to cook. She had a son named Robby that was away at college but came home on the weekends. I tried to help around the house, the best that I could. I spent a lot of time alone in my bedroom.

This one-day Mrs. Thompson and I had it out as she wanted me to kill a chicken for dinner and I was not having it. I would not kill the chickens that I fed every day. So, I left the house and walked to a playground nearby. No one was there, and I sat down and cried my eyes out. I tried to stop, but the tears just kept flowing like a faucet had been turned on. I looked up at heaven and told God that I did not know what to do. I walked home and did not say anything and went to my room. The next day she never mentioned what had happened and did not ask me to kill any more chickens.

That was the day Robby her son came home from college. He was such a nice guy. We had pizza that night, and things did not seem so bad. He took the time to talk to me as if I were a real person and what I had to say, mattered. His mother said that we were going to spend three days up in New Hampshire on a lake. They had a nice log cabin up there, and since it was the beginning of Fall it would be a beautiful time to go. All the leaves would have already started to change color, making it a spectacle to behold. I was so excited about going. I felt like I might really be a part of this family. When we arrived at the lake, it was just as beautiful as I had imagined. It was like looking at a beautiful painting with swirls of orange, yellow, red, green, and brown, surrounded by patches of blue sky overlooking the bluish almost turquoise water. It was breathtaking, and the air was crisp and clean with the scent of burning wood from the fireplaces.

Even the fir trees added their own sweetness. We quickly unpacked, because it was late, and we were all tired and hungry. After we ate, we unrolled our sleeping bags on the cabin floor. As we sat next to a warm crackling fire in a stone-built fireplace we sang songs. Then we all curled up in our sleeping bags, in this one big wooden room with wooden floors and went to sleep. I remember thinking that it could not ever get much better than this. The next day Robby said to me, *"Do you want to take a walk around the lake?"* I replied, *"Okay."* We asked his Mom and she said, sure, but be back soon. Robby had one bad leg that was weak, so he did not walk fast. Every once and awhile we had to sit down so that he could rest his leg. We lost track of time because we talked about our lives. Robby treated me just like a little sister and he seemed to have great compassion when I told him my story. He told me that I needed to value myself more and not give in to everyone else's needs, but to understand what was right for me. I cherished every word that he said. This day spent with Robby was incredibly special and it would always hold an incredibly special place in my heart. We stopped for a while, sitting on a log next to the lake giving off a mirrored reflection of the trees, while the puffy white clouds floated above the crystal-clear blue water. The leaves fell all around us in a feeling of poetic peace. I wanted to make time stop, but the darkness of the night was slowly surrounding us.

By the time we got back to the cabin it was already dark, and Mrs. Thompson was wild. She started accusing us of having had sex in the woods. Robby came to our defense, but she was not having it. She looked at me and said, *"We are leaving tomorrow morning, and just as soon as I can arrange it, you are going back to the state, Missy."*

I replied with tears flowing down my face, "But I didn't do anything wrong." She shook her fist at me and said, "That remains to be seen. Who knows what you two have done? You have both been gone way too long. You have both been gone for hours, and I'm not going to put up with a little tramp like you."

Robby looked at me as if he were in shock, and I knew I didn't belong there. I went to bed without anything to eat.

The next day came, and we all packed, but not one of us spoke, as there was an eerie silence. It felt like if someone spoke the world would crack and come tumbling down. When we got back, Robby had to go back to school. His mom forbade him to say goodbye to me, but he came over to me just before he left and said, "Sandy, forgive us, *I'm so sorry.*"

I replied, *"Don't worry about me. I will be just fine."* It took every ounce of strength for me not to break down and cry.

Robby bent over and kissed me on my cheek, and said, *"You are not what my mother said, and there is nothing in this life that could ever make me believe that about you. Good luck, Sandy. I only wish I were able to help you."* As he walked away, I stood there in the driveway and imagined I was building a brick wall up around myself. This imaginary brick wall felt real, and it was there to protect me.

LIFE WITH THE MINISTER'S FAMILY

The next day I walked down to the Methodist church. I told the minister I needed a home, and if he knew of anyone in the church that would not mind me staying with them, it would be greatly appreciated. Otherwise, the state could put me anywhere and I would be pulled out of school and must start over someplace else. I gave him the name of the doctor who knew me, so that if he found someone the doctor could help me to be put there. The minister Reverend Stiers gave me lots of hope and said that he had two little children that needed someone to live in and take care of them while he and his wife were busy with school, church, and seminars. He said that he would talk it over with his wife Brenda and let me know the very next day if I could come and live with them.

Life with the Minister's Family I knew Mrs. Thompson did not really hate me, but she saw that her son liked me, and she did not want that to go any further than she felt it already did. She had eliminated the threat, which in her eyes and mind was me. No matter what has ever happened to me in my life, there has always been this strong force protecting me. Sometimes it has felt so strong that I felt like I could almost reach out and touch it. I had desired to go live with the minister and his family, and it happened. The very next day the doctor came to take me to my new foster home. Rev. Stiers, his wife Brenda, and their two little girls, Heather and Gretchen, had a beautiful home in a country setting. There was even a swing hanging over a babbling brook. The perfect little family in a perfectly gorgeous setting. Somehow this all seemed too perfect for me to be a part of, but I was going to do my absolute best. They welcomed me in with open arms. I guess I did not look too threatening, holding tight to my small suitcase, all ninety three pounds of me.

Rev. Stiers replied, *"Okay, maybe you would like Brenda to show you to your room."*

I replied, *"Yes, I would like that very much."*

Brenda and I went upstairs to my new bedroom. It was the most beautiful room in the whole wide world. It was exceptionally large, in an L-shape, a full-size bed with lots of pretty pillows. The furniture was a light ash wood with cream-colored walls, and all the accents were pink, yellow, and a light green. Where the room ended in this L-shape corner there was a beautiful chest that you could sit on by the window. I even had my own bathroom, and I was in a different part of the house than everyone else. I was upstairs and there was a den across from my room, but everyone else lived and slept downstairs. It was my very own little haven from the world. This was too much to even hope for, but here it was. I wanted to jump up & down and scream for joy, but I acted very quiet and calm until Brenda left the room for me to unpack, at which moment I flung myself onto my new bed and was covered in pretty pillows. Just before she had left her words were still singing in my mind, *"Sandy, I hope you like your new room, new home and especially your new family. I want you to know you can come to us anytime and talk to us about anything. This is your new home now and we want you to be happy here. When you get ready, please come downstairs, because we will be having dinner shortly."*

I had thanked Brenda for letting me stay there and told her I would try to do my best to fit in with the family. At that she smiled and walked away. I wanted to hug her but felt that would all come in time.

I remember this as the most blessed time in my life. I went to high school, belonged to the pilgrim fellowship youth group attending all the church retreats and activities, attended church every Sunday, joined the Rainbow Girls as my Uncles were 32nd & honorary 33rd degree Mason of the Masonic Order along with my mother who was an Eastern Star, and I had friends my age and people that I could relate too. God had put me in a place to grow spiritually and a place to be safe, in a million years what more could I have wanted or needed at that time in my life. Even the minister's mother & father that came from Minnesota wanted to adopt me, but when I turned sixteen, I returned home to my mother to help her. I worked at the Southern New England Telephone Company and went to school. I could never be able to repay Rev. Thomas Stiers and his wife Brenda for their beautiful hearts filled with so much kindness.

"I STAND ALONE"

Twisted lives and mangled hearts,
In deepest darkness are apart.
The air feels thick dense hard to breathe, an enormous hole of
emptiness inside of me.
I feel no love, I harbor no hate,
Yet so much pain eats my soul, destroys my fate
What lies ahead are only shadows of the dawn,
waiting only to dance upon the lives that have gone.
Searching for a spark of life inside of me, Desperately needing
hope to let my soul soar free,
Torn, stripped, fearful at six years old, Treated like a demon
sentenced to the cold
Pretending to love cherish and adore,
My doll, or was it me, who really needed more?
So long ago, so very long ago.
There is no pity or tears left to show.
I feel safe now within my walls of grief. Dare not happiness show
itself even brief
The waves of pain flow over me.
From head to toe agony won't let me be.
I know why God turns away,
For the ones he loves, hurt him day by day,
It's not safe to trust, believe, love, or care,
Heaven forbid your life you do share
I can't believe the anger and despair I know,
I seem to be nurturing it, helping it grow.
In desperation, I cling to my friends, time and space,
a look of hollow dreams upon my face. The day is breaking
black as night,
All around evil rejoices in pleasured fright

Don't try to run, climb or hide,
Stop-be still- you can't escape the fear inside.
Only cold silence will hear your screams, You want to sleep but,
scared to dream.
You know what waits for you in sleep, Savage thoughts
in Monster
Shapes stalk and creep.
Your thoughts keep turning around and around,
You can't seem to quiet the roaring sound.
By Sandy Olson

MY CO-WORKER'S DREAM

I was working at TRW Geometric Tool in Westville, Connecticut. I had a co-worker come up to me one day and appear in some sort of strange awe about me. He said that he would always be there to help me if I ever needed help, because of a dream he had about me the night before. He knew that I was happily married so I did not take his comment as flirtation. I asked him to tell me about his dream.

He said he was walking in the woods and it felt as if God was with him. He saw a catholic nun walking ahead of him, he wanted to see if she needed any help, but by the time he came close to her she was already walking on the other side of the river into the woods. He went to great trouble to cross the stream and when he caught up to the nun, he put his hand upon her shoulder. He said that he was in total shock when she turned around to look at him, because the nun was me.

I really don't know what to say about that, but his intentions to protect me seemed real.

CO-WORKER'S VISIT FROM AN ANGEL

About twenty-five years later I was selling Real estate and I worked with an underwriter to help get my loans through for many clients. He would always tell me what they needed to do, to qualify them for a mortgage. I sometimes would drop off paperwork at his home as his wife was doing all the secretarial work for him. Usually I would only see her. He was always very business-like, and I never knew if he was religious or not, as we only spoke about work. This one day I dropped by with a big folder of papers for his wife to go through. As I was talking to her at a counter that was used for business in their house, he walked by me and stopped abruptly, looked at me and said, "An angel visited me last night and wanted me to give you a message." I looked at him as if he were telling me a joke and I was waiting for the punchline. *"He wanted me to tell you that there is a crown of stars awaiting you in heaven."* I smiled, and he just turned and walked away. I looked at his wife and said, *"I've never seen him kid around before."* Then to my astonishment she replied, *"He wasn't."* She said, *"It has only happened a couple of times, but an angel really did come to visit him."* I did not know what to say, so we just continued with the file that I had brought her to work on. I could not find out what receiving a crown of stars meant, not even in the bible, but many years later I came across its meaning. It was said, long before the bible came to be. It was an ancient belief that if someone was considered a good soul, that when they died, they were given a crown of stars in heaven as an honor for their goodness upon the earth.

EXTRATERRESTRIAL VISITORS

It was near the very end of September 1978 and you might take note that the previous month I had a prophetic dream unfold on the day the Pope and my grandmother died. This would prove to be the most haunting night of my life. This night would forever leave me with more questions than I could ever answer. Although I don't see it as a curse, but rather a blessing in understanding that we are truly not alone on many levels in many ways. This night started out like most every night, home from work, dinner, and then the family settled down for a little TV. Then out of nowhere the nightly routine began to change. I made a point of never going out late at night, especially since we had a couple of people that had been mugged in our parking lot, but not even fear or caution would stop the events that were to unfold. I got up, walked into the kitchen, opened the refrigerator door, and looked in. For some reason, I did not see the gallon container of milk that was half full sitting right there in plain sight. I then walked into the living room and told my husband that I was going out to get some milk. He started arguing with me about not having done this earlier and complaining about not having milk in his coffee to start the day. My girls chimed in, and they wanted to go too. Susan was twelve and Candy was eight years old. At first, I thought it was too late to bring them with me, as it was around nine thirty, and they needed to get ready for bed. Then I thought they could run in for me quickly when I pulled up to the market, so I said, *"OK."* It was a cool night, and the sky was clear lit with stars. We headed for the market like we had done a million times before, Stop-n-Shop over by the Merritt Parkway. We drove under the parkway and immediately took a left over by Stop-n Shop, which was now on our right. Instead of stopping I drove right by the market and was incredibly surprised that I had done that. Now I would have to make a big circle to go back, because the lane I was in only went one way around the parking lot. This was a large lot, so it would take me a few minutes to go back, I decided to take a short cut and went across the middle of the lot instead of staying in the main lane. I had taken a left and was intending to take another left at the end of the lane, then take another left to circle back to the market. Before we reached the end of the lane that we were crossing, which was in the middle of a parking lot, we all looked up and saw this very big ship silently hovering about three stories high over the Merritt Parkway. It was an incredible sight to behold, causing me to stop the car immediately. We didn't know what kind of an aircraft it was. The hull on top & bottom was like a shiny pewter. The middle had exceptionally large windows that were separated by the same metal of the ship, like large metal beams in-between the glass windows. Lights in a spectrum of color appeared to be traveling clockwise around the middle of the ship. There was a large dome light on top of the ship. The ship was concave on top and bottom in a saucer type shape with the ends cut off or oblong shape with the ends cut straight off. The very bottom of the ship was flat. It was tremendous in size, and I wondered how it could just be hovering there so quietly. There were lots of cars coming from the direction of New York City, which was north of us, and they would have pulled over if they had been able to see the ship. They were coming down the side of a mountain that would have brought them to eye level with the ship, so they were unable to see it. At first, I thought this must be something our Air Force was testing, or maybe we had driven into an area where they were filming a movie, I quickly glanced around looking for cameras. As I glanced there were people in the background, but nobody was looking up. I wanted to get out the car and scream *"look up, look up!"* but I couldn't. Candy was next to me in the middle of the front seat, and Susan was by the door. They started pushing and shoving each other, saying we are being invaded. I turned to them and said, *"Stop that! They are friendly,"* Just as fast as the words came out of my mouth, I realized I didn't know what made me say that. How would I know if they were friendly? Then I looked up at the ship and had a feeling that they were saying goodbye. The ship started to slowly head toward downtown New Haven & I said to the girls should we follow it and we all answered *"No"* at the same time. Just as we saw the ship start to pull away, I noticed there were no cars on the parkway anymore. Even the shopping center was deserted, and the Stop-n-Shop was closed. Only the night lights were left on in the stores. I thought, *"How could everyone disappear so quickly?"* We lost several hours, as it was almost twelve o'clock by the time we got home. We didn't know at first that we had been taken aboard the ship. We drove away, looking for some store that would still be open. We did find a 24- hour place and picked up the milk. When we had arrived home my husband was frantic with worry. He *said "What took you so long? The eleven o'clock news is over, and they were telling about blackouts all over the city. Even our apartment building experienced a complete blackout."* We looked totally calm, and answered, *"It didn't feel like we were gone more than ten minutes, Oh, by the way we saw this strange looking spaceship."* We acted like it was really nothing important, and I went to put the milk away in the refrigerator only to find milk already there. We didn't need to go out at all that night. I thought how strange that was, then immediately dismissed the thought. As a matter of fact, that continued to happen each time one of us remembered something from that night. We would acknowledge it or say it, then immediately dismiss it. This became common practice for years regarding that night. The next day there were reports in New York and Connecticut of UFO sightings.

Even a mother with her two daughters claimed that they saw a spaceship go by their windows of their apartment which was in a New York City skyscraper. An East Haven police officer who was out on the back roads in North Branford also reported seeing the space craft, but within a few hours after several reports were made all news of this spaceship were silenced. My daughter came to me the next day after the sighting and showed me this large blood red mark on her lower leg. It looked like a large piece of skin had been removed from the shin area, but the area appeared healed. We acknowledge it, then never brought it up again. I had a surgical blood red scar ¾" on my left leg, on the left side of my knee. I also felt like there was something in my nose, way up inside and I kept trying to blow it out as it was uncomfortable. I finally did and it was a small hard round thing that looked like a tiny ball bearing covered in flesh. I dismissed it and threw it away after showing a co-worker. I had dreams about the incident, and I had feelings about what happened, not memories. I felt I had been terrified on the ship and I started to pray, this alien with large eyes spoke to my mind. He touched my forehead gently and said, *"He is our God too."*

The strangest part of this entire event is two weeks before I had this extraterrestrial encounter, I had prayed begging God to let me know if there were other beings in our universe. Shall we call it a coincidence, if so, it must be one of those rare one's. Also, you must note that other people connected to that night have come up to me throughout my life and out of nowhere start telling me about their encounter, but only a handful. They only thought it was just a sighting. Space is not Empty, It is Filled with Answers.

DREAM AFTER ENCOUNTER

Then I had a dream I was trying to get away from them, I crossed a dark river then came to a house, I told my daughter we must go as they are here, but she stayed. I ran into a barn and hid among the bales of hay. It was very quiet, so I decided to come out and when I did, they were all quietly standing there. My head hung down, then I asked, *"How did you find me?"* He walked over to me, picking up my hand then turning it over you could see the palm of my hand glowing green, I woke up. I really don't know what to tell you about all of this, only that there is a whole lot more to our existence than we are aware of. Also, Bud Hopkins contacted me from MUFON, my mother received the call saying, that I didn't want to talk to them, strangely enough I had never said that to her, but I ended up moving and never met with them anyway.

MOLECULAR CHANGE

My visit with God displayed his power to easily manipulate matter & energy. He made a cloud silently light up with electrical energy, then caused that energy to flow slowly out of the cloud with the consistency of water solidifying as it wrote upon the sky, just like ink upon a piece of paper. Which brings me to something I haven't fully been able to comprehend. I was bringing my four grandchildren back home. The oldest was in the front seat, the other three were in the back seat. We were in this tiny car called a Vega. I needed to cross six lanes to get to the other side. I looked to my left and saw a car traveling slowly so I thought that I could cross. I didn't see the car that was far down the road behind that car which was moving about 65-70 mph. Just as I pulled out into the second lane, I saw a large Lincoln Continental almost at my window. The front width of this car appeared almost as big as the entire length of my car. I froze realizing it might try to go around me even though that possibility seemed too late, as his car was moving too fast and was too close. Everything seemed to feel like it went into slow motion, I thought the car did not get around the front of my car, but that would mean the car passed through the front of my car. As I turned my head looking out the other window the car was still in my lane and I was watching it from behind speed down the road. I told my daughter when I got to her house if I didn't know it was impossible, I would think a car changed from matter to energy in a split second then back to matter. If that car had hit us, we would have all been killed. A couple of weeks went by and my daughter called me and said, *"you know that car possibly passing through your car, well a woman and her children just reported that they experienced that in St. Pete."* This was strange especially since that wasn't far from where this happened to me and my grandchildren. God has total control over all things in this universe and energy connects us all. Now that I am putting all the pieces together from my life, I can only tell you that I have a very unusual collection of pieces. Which would explain my very unusual reasoning behind most subjects.

MINISTER'S MIRACLE, METHODIST
CHURCH NEAR YALE UNIVERSITY

In the late 80's, I met this genuinely nice minister who had a beautiful church across from the New Haven green, right near Yale University. He had the pilgrim fellowship youth group from his church come to my house to help me stack a pile of rocks that were in my backyard to make way for an in- ground pool. I can tell you New England has a lot of rocks. I went in to make the young people hot chocolate and invited the minister in for a cup of coffee. We were talking about faith when suddenly, he felt compelled to share a very unusual experience that he had recently had. He said that his congregation would ship him off to an island if he shared it with them, but he felt that he could share it with me.

His wife had muscular-dystrophy and when he laid her down in bed at night she could not sit up again on her own. He had walked over to their bedroom window as he had done many nights to say a prayer for her. He asked God to please make it possible for her to be able to sit up at least one more time. He looked over at her, and the covers on the bed were moving as her skeleton sat straight up in the bed, then her organs came up to be with her skeleton, then her skin came up and covered her body, and there she sat straight up in the bed. She never opened her eyes, but God had answered his prayer. I could see a sense of relief that he had been able to share that with someone that would not judge him with their disbelief. I can tell you I truly know how he felt. Don't worry about making others believe you, as long as you can believe, know that your Creator knows the truth and he is all that matters. That is the only one you will ever truly need, when it comes to knowing who you truly are. When he is with you, who can be against you. For God created all things through His holy active force of energy and just as He turned energy into matter, He has the power to control every atom that is in every molecule.

HOMELESS MAN

I drove into a parking lot and saw a man sitting on a curb with a dog. The man was very thin & bony with rags for clothes. Every once and awhile the man would lift his glasses as if he were really hiding behind them. Everyone passed by him and his dog and they did not even see them. It was an extremely hot day and the dog looked like he needed water. The dog started to walk away and was limping a little bit and the man got up and followed his dog, looking as if the dog was the owner of the man. I stopped my car and walked up to them and asked the man, "what can I do for you?" He said, *"We need food, and my dog likes meat."* I said, *"OK, I'll get you something."* I walked into the store grabbing big pre- made sandwiches, containers of meat, a gallon of water & a bowl to put the water in for the dog. I didn't have much money left in my account, but I took it out. When I came out, they were sitting by the wall of the market within this small crevice of shade. I gave him the food, water, and money. He lifted his glasses and his eyes seemed to sparkle when he said, *"Watch out for August 17th something bad is coming."* I thought he was referring to the end as so many people do. So, I smiled back and said, *"I'll see you on the other side."* Then he smiled too. He didn't say what year, or even what will happen, and it is now August 2017, I only hope it is not this August. Time will tell.

On August 17, 2017 in Barcelona, Spain a terrorist attack occurred killing 14 people, out of another more than 120 injured 17 out of that remain in critical condition. This may just be a coincidence, but you never know for sure.

MIRACLES COME FROM BELIEVING

There was this woman in the bible that had been very sick for a long time and she grew weaker and weaker. She had heard that Jesus was coming to the place where she lived. She had heard about His many miracles healing people and she believed with all her heart if she just touched the edge of His garment that she too would be healed. So as sick as she was when He came, He was surrounded by a multitude of people, but she pushed herself through the crowd even in pain as she knew He could help her. The last several feet she had to crawl through the crowd, and then she touched the edge of His garment and was immediately healed. He said, *"Who has touched me,"* for He had felt the healing flow from His body. She was scared but admitted that it was her. *"Take heart daughter,"* He said, *"Your faith has healed you."* We say we believe, but many times we immediately doubt the blessings & miracles that others have received and even doubt our own blessings. We try to rationalize what is beyond our understanding while we are here as physical beings. It is the doubt that the universe responds to, it is the doubt that stops your blessings. I was trying to help take care of many of my family members and I needed some financial help at the time. I had just started a small business and I knew with all my heart if I could mail out this box of advertisement that I had, that I could make the money that I needed. I was sitting outside a convenience store and the box was on the seat next to me. It would cost exactly three hundred dollars to pay to mail out this box of advertisement. Now I know like you know God does not necessarily help us to win at gambling, but I very seldom played a lotto ticket and just about never played a scratch off ticket, but desperate times call for desperate measures.

I looked up at the sky, placing my hand on top of the post cards and said, *"God you know my situation and I need to mail these cards, I promise if you help me to get three hundred dollars I will go straight to the Post Office and mail these cards."* So, I went in and played my last dollar with the expectancy that God would make this happen if He chose too. I went back to the car knowing that no matter what happened God loved me and there was no doubt in my mind about that. I scratched off the ticket and it was exactly three hundred dollars. I walked back into the store collected my money, went to the Post Office and mailed my advertising post cards. I received work for years off those post cards. God is always there for us, but we must be willing to accept His blessings and not constantly doubt the greatest power in the universe.

Reach out to this universal power and He will never forsake you, but it will be what He knows is right for you, even if it is hard for you to understand. For God always sees the bigger picture and He loves you dearly.

(PART OF) DAUGHTER'S
DREAM CROSSING OVER

She arrived on a platform in Heaven after a bad accident and there was a doorway on the other side behind her and her husband as they stepped into a place where she immediately felt at home. The place was white, there was a conductor there that was telling her to get ready to go back to the physical world, but she refused to go back as she knew her family would also come to this side. She knew that she would meet them again when it was their time to cross over. She felt that this is where she wanted to be in a place that filled her being with a completeness with a sense of overwhelming happiness and joy. Her husband appeared younger than her by a few years and he said, that he was going to go find a friend that he knew, so he left to go find his friend and she felt good about that as they were now home. She was no longer a woman in her late forties, she appeared to be 23 years old, then she woke up.

I have had similar dreams with God and just like her I felt that overwhelming completeness, belonging, and love. There is no doubt in my mind that this physical life is a place where we come to learn, experience, and understand. We all come into this world from the other side, we all leave this world & return to our true self, which is a spiritual energy, we are all one humanity, under one God that is an indestructible power. Have a good heart & be a beacon of hope for all those to see while you are here visiting this physical world.

DREAMS REFLECTING THE END

The first, presence of evil I was standing in a room, but I could clearly see the outside. Blue sky, green rolling hills, trees, and the illumination of light, everything else in the room was white as if there was no end. I was standing in what appeared to be an oblong circle. There were three Mideastern rugs to my right and three to my left, they were not touching each other, but formed the sides of the oblong circle. A man in white robes entered the room and stood directly across from me completing the circle. The moment he entered I realized that he was pure evil, and fear ran through my body and it felt paralyzing. Then six male human beings entered the room, each one sitting upon a rug. I looked to my right at the man on the first rug next to the evil man in white robes, his skin started to roll off his body, then his muscles, organs, blood along with his bones melting down the sides, and emerging out of his body came forth a leopard. The leopard looked straight at me and chills ran down my spine. The leopard curled around then sat straight up on the first rug. The second man began to change, and the skin, muscles, blood, organs and bone melted away from his body and a bear emerged, I quickly looked at the man next to me on my right side, as the third animal emerged which was a boar with protruding tusks out of his mouth that appeared like horns. To my left the animal emerged giving a loud roar for it was a lion and the next animal had already started to come out, but I looked to my left and ran for the door that appeared on the white wall. No sooner had I closed the door behind me when I noticed the evil man in white robes was still standing across from me the very same distance that he had stood across from me in the circle. Then I woke up. I don't know the whole meaning yet, but I think this is some of it. The man in white is who we refer to as the Antichrist, I couldn't escape him even when I left the room, because he is in our world. The rugs signify the countries around Israel, that will rise against her. The animals were the leaders, two of which I didn't see come out as I had

78

already run for the door. For some reason I was not supposed to know who those last two leaders were. So, this is the beginning of something horrible.

The visions that God showed me are coming true. God showed me what was going to happen in our world before the end which will be our Beginning. He showed me the Leopard which was Afghanistan pushing us out of their country by the Taliban while we were trying to leave. He showed me the Bear rising up which is Russia that has come against Ukraine in a Great War, the next animal was the Boar which stands for Ukraine having been attacked by the Bear. Ukraine's culture came from the Celtic Tribes and the Boar represented the symbol of their god, standing for Valor, Ferocious Strength for the warrior and it was their most popular animal symbol. Ukraine & Poland have always embraced the Wild Boar & Pig, as a sign of Prosperity, Success, & Material Wealth. The Germanic People of Ukraine felt the Boar was a Powerful symbol. Even my vision showed the Boar with 3 Tusks just like their symbol. The Lion that roared stands for Finland, for when they saw what was happening to Ukraine they roared loudly in order to join the United Nations.

Recently I had a vision when Russia came against Ukraine and I saw a pit of total darkness, giant chains glimmering in blackness, skeletons descending into the pit, landing within the openings of the chains, as the chains turned breaking the bones into pieces. I saw the fate of our wicked then I remembered when I was taken to our Beginning. Acts 2:17 is upon us now.

After my skeleton vision, I found an ancient biblical text; Behold the end of human greatness now; Low to the dust is laid the lofty brow;

Of princely pride, a skeleton remains; Tis common dust. The broken sword & chains; That once enslaved mankind have lost their power; Broken the glass that told of his triumph hour.

I had written "God's Visit" by Sandy Olson, in 2017 which was before all these things started to play out. Showing that these Prophecies came before the events.

THE DIVIDING

I think this dream is very symbolic, but I'm not sure. I was standing in front of an enormous pit many city blocks in depth and length, the bottom of this pit appeared endless. As I stood there, I saw people falling into the pit and their faces were horribly distorted with fear. I looked up and saw the people being thrown out of an extremely high skyscraper, there were no windows on that floor of the building where they were being thrown out. The floor that they were being thrown out was three stories down from the top of the building (meaning if the building was 100 stories high, they were being thrown out of the 97thfloor). All the people were being gathered into this building and were being pushed to walk up the stairway towards the floor where people were being thrown out. They also pushed me into the building, and we were all moving up the staircase like crammed in sardines. We didn't seem to have a choice. Just before I got to the top, I reached my hand out to my family so that we could go together. I said to them lets hold hands making a chain and don't let go. When I stepped on the landing of the floor there were two giant men in front of me, I thought that they were giant angels. The angel on the right went to take me to the window where the people were being thrown out, but the angel to the right of him crossed his arm in front of the angel reaching for me and said, "no, not this one." Then that angel led me down a hallway as my whole family never broke the chain of hands. He opened a door that opened into a giant auditorium and we went in only to observe there were only a few other families huddling together in different parts of this giant space. I realized that most of the other people were going into the pit.

I woke up. I think there is a dividing taking place right now among the people, as I noticed there are a lot of religious groups that are not acting on the side of goodness and humanity, but seem to be following the wickedness that has entered our world. The deceiver can easily deceive those who are not pure in heart. I implore you not to follow religion but follow what goodness you can find in your heart right now.

Religions have always been a moral compass for mankind, but right now the compass may be pointing in the wrong direction and the only way you can test it is through love, compassion, goodness, tolerance, understanding, forgiveness, kindness, caring, selflessness, and above all ask God himself for guidance. He Hears You, He Will Not Fail You, His will shall be done on earth, as in heaven.

As I walk toward the light of God I feel His love; I feel His peace surrounding me with gentle snow white doves; His voice is calming, deep, and clear; His presence is an energy that I can feel & hear; I'm home within His arms, No more fear of being harmed.

THE SIXTH TRUMP-ET

We may be facing the worst time in the history of humanity. You know the old saying, if you keep crying wolf one day when the wolf really comes no one will believe you. I feel humanity is ready to go to another level of physical being, a new kind of life, one of great peace, understanding and a true joy in the sense of living. A new humanity that will enjoy being human and a physical being that will be totally free from all the deep hatreds and wickedness. Every coin will still have two sides, just like every story, but the extreme will be gone on both sides. That brings me to where we are now, I can't make up my mind as to whether it is John The Trump-Et who will be ushering our fall or if he is making way for the real silent killer. Even Christ was preceded by John The Baptist.

I must stop here to acknowledge the John The Trump-Et voters, they see John The Trump-Et as a savior that will either give them what they need or bring it back into their lives. The man that is not afraid of anything or anyone. Like the golden calf that the Israelites worshiped in the desert to bring them back to the bondage of Egypt, just so they would be certain about their prospects even if that meant living as slaves, they would still be taken care of. This rings a familiar note, just give us back our coal mines we don't need to learn a new way. He is so much like the golden calf, the man who comes down from his golden tower, to offer the masses a sense of power, but just like the golden calf that has no heart, he will only lead them into serving his needs and providing their destruction. Then there is the correlation that many who have been deceived have strong religious ties, and for the sake of what they want, the golden calf fits right into what they believe God wants for them. To that they would say, *"how do you know what God wants for us? do you think you are God?"*

Thank God, I'm not God, as I would Not have the patience to listen to their nonsense. Unlike God, who even cares about his most wicked children, and would listen to them no matter how far they have strayed, if they just reach out to him or call upon his name. November 2016, after the presidential election, the sixth trumpet sounded over Israel, and as we know there are only seven that will sound before the end of humanity as we know it.

Someone said to me, isn't it strange his name is trump-et, maybe he is the sixth trumpet, but there is no need for instant alarm, as there will more than likely be a great deal of suffering before the evil that has come into this world will let us off the hook. The bad boy The Sixth Trump-ET certainly fits the description, a liar, a person of great deception, someone who appears god-like to his followers (I can kill someone on the street and not lose a single vote). A man without ethics, amoral in attitude, immoral in actions, someone who taunts us with his smirk like grin of I can do anything, and you can't stop me. I'm sure his followers find that exhilarating to be able to say F-You, to the establishment. Or is he just setting us up for an even greater evil that is the antichrist waiting in the wings to come out into the world and deceive us all.

Someone with a magnetic personality, a person who shows great power, intelligence, and an ability to bring us together after the bad boy Sixth Trumpet is gone. Someone who has an agenda so wickedly devastating we will never see it coming or even know what hit us.

We are now swimming in murky waters not knowing who we can really trust, here upon this earth. I wish I had the answer, but just like you I am going to have to watch it all play out. Those who are truly with God, I can only say with all my heart, stay faithful to the end. I can only believe that God will give us the strength that we will need to do that. The tests will be hard and at times the lines between right and wrong will be unclear. Hold onto that goodness in your heart and it will not fail you. Try to stay around like-minded people, as I fear much like the Sixth Trumpet administration's chaos we are not going to know up from down or left from right. Truth will be surrounded by the light of goodness, while deception will be deep within the darkness of lies.

Tweet:

I saw a pretty parakeet of many colors, surrounded by a darkness of crows billowing their hate for the little parakeet of many colors, I thought the parakeet is our Democracy which is in danger and the crows were the present political administration of 2018 doing anything no matter how despicable in order to get what they want and bleed the country dry, and at that moment this is what came to mind.

"Pretty little parakeet just wanted to be free, Pretty little parakeet flew out into a tree, The crows were flying swarming all around, Now pretty little parakeets are nowhere to be found."

(Let's not lose our Democracy, for that is the part of our government that stands for us, the people)

It has taken me a long time, but I finally understand my Dividing dream. Just before the people came to stand before the Giant Angels that appeared as Giant men, their appearance is spoken of in an Egyptian interpretation of the Revelations.

I realize now that we were not spared, because of me. The giant man saw that we were a group of people holding hands in Unity. It is this Unity that will save many. We are presently in the Dividing stage of Revelation. God needs us to know that during this Dividing stage, in order for us to survive what is to come we need Unity. Right now, we are being torn apart by the Greedy, & Hateful. They tell us what to think, and what we need, they use us by Dividing us because if we are United, they can't control us collectively. We need to pull together by putting any differences aside. God showed me that the ones that will survive will create a link holding hands. Put aside your Hate & following people who want you to serve their needs. Especially the ones who want to rule us, not represent us, but drain as much as they can from us. God was right the people have been blinded & cannot see the truth! Read "The End Is Our Beginning" by Sandy Olson then just pass it on. It's not about money it is about understanding what we are facing and standing together. God loves you so very much & as He has come upon many, He will come upon You. Know that you are not alone.

PURIFYING THE WORLD FROM EVIL

My Daughter one who believes in many things and many truths had a Dream/Vision. She was walking up a hill and there was this mountain on top of the hill that soared high into the sky.

The mountain was made out of human bodies placed in a spiraling pattern all the way to the top.

The mountain of bodies was on fire, burning so hot that the skeletons were charred white in ashes.

One skeleton's head was hanging over the side of the pattern charred white. Her Grand-daughter was walking behind her and she became fearful that her Grand-daughter might breathe in this evil, infected tainted smoke-filled air.

Then she woke up. We are all being tainted and infected by these wicked times. We all know deep inside what is truly happening, even for those that have been blinded to the truth.

Our only hope is Faith, Love, & Unity

THERE IS HOPE

I dreamt that I was riding along this road and God's voice told me to get into a house, any house. I stopped the car and took refuge in this small house built upon a slab of concrete. The foundation of the house started to lift off the ground and the whole house leaned forward, and I could see the ground from the large living room windows. I was above the state of Florida and I could see the entire peninsula being covered by a tidal wave only leaving a small piece of land left underwater up by the Panhandle. Eventually the house sat down in a wheat field and the house opened like a flower peeling back it's petals. I walked out and saw other houses landing in the wheat field and those houses that appeared structured like Pod Shaped Spacecraft landing. I saw the people walk out of those houses fall to their knees and pray. I fell to my knees too, as this was a new beginning for all of us.

When the Russians started the war against Ukraine, I dreamt I walked into a room filled with body parts. When I left the room I told someone don't go in there it is filled with snakes. I've been receiving visions/ dreams for a long time & they are now starting to play out in the world. I saw our Eastern seaboard hit by Tidal waves & Russia has Nuclear missiles that create tidal waves & Putin has already been testing them. Florida was completely wiped out. Don't be blinded the world is presently walking through the book of Revelations.

The trump-et has sounded announcing the Hatred and Evil that has come upon the world. John the trump-et will bow before the Son of Evil anointing him as Lord of Darkness. The trump-et will embrace Russia and the world Dictators, for he has opened the door to Armageddon. As the End comes upon his followers they will be dismayed, but it will be too late. For they have chosen Hate over Love. It is never too late to stand up for what is right.

86

We have all heard about the news of Armageddon, and the end of our world, but my dream is telling me that it is not an end, but a beginning for humanity through their own will to come closer to the will of Creation. We will have to face many hardships and many demons, but if you remain faithful in your heart, holding onto goodness for the sake of righteousness, you will know a world of true peace. God Bless you and be with you always. "As for my house, we serve the Lord.'

CONNECTING THE DOTS

Just as I promised we are going to connect the dots in order to understand why I now believe the way I do, as my thoughts seem to be very disturbing to most people, especially to the religious. People will say to me things like "what bible are you reading?" in a sarcastic tone. Well, that is an honest question, but if we are going to be completely truthful our Christian bible originally came from divinely inspired books written in Hebrew and Aramaic, put together by fourth century opinion and sixth century priests that determined what books they felt were divinely prophesied. Keeping in mind their teachings and the need to keep out anything that would undermine their influence over us. Any books that were considered liberating to the masses certainly wouldn't have been chosen even though they were divinely inspired. I will take it one step further in saying, I believe we can safely say God the creator was not going to entrust humanity with the secrets of the universe. That would have been like giving baby riches instead of food.

I started out at five years old with my out of body experience floating above a dead self without a clue in the world what had just happened. Only a few minutes in-between this life and the next. Could such an experience have started all the supernatural events, probably not, but it could have made me more aware of all the spirits around me. Then let's filter in that strange experience my mother had with me when I was first born in Albuquerque, New Mexico. Waking up to this strange giant aircraft seemingly blocking out the sun above us, silently hovering over us, then quickly disappearing. Could we connect the extraterrestrial encounter in Westville, Ct. by the Merritt Parkway with that? Possibly.

Then we have the strange dreams, four of them powerfully connected with God and Christ in my twenties. Two of the dreams with clouds, just like Ethel had mentioned to me many years before.

We could have possibly concurred it was her reference to a Godly visit that triggered them, except for the fact that one of the dreams unfolded after I woke up, playing out step by step including witnessing an impossible sky that has never been seen again in my life time nor have I ever seen pictures of such a sky that absolutely mirrored the sky in the dream. On the very day that Pope Paul VI had died, such a strange coincidence. A man considered high ranking in religion somehow connected with a dream where God spoke to me, and on the day that an incredible sky would appear at the very given moment it appeared in the dream. Mind boggling to say the least. Then later in life dreams become prophecies and play out, along with more prophecies to be fulfilled in our near future to come.

Let us connect an event that appeared to have been matter turning into energy instantly then back to matter. Then God manifested in this world turning energy into matter then back to energy. I ask you how on earth can I possibly see things as we have been taught, when my life was never in the box of the so-called norm to begin with. People may be confused about my conclusions, but I must share them as we are evolving into the next steps of why we exist in the first place. We touched on this a little bit already, but considering the complexity, we will touch on it again for the sake of connecting dots. When my friend experienced her present life overlapping with another time, the possibilities just blew my mind, but beyond any shadow of doubt I believe in what I am going to say to you about the possibilities that this represents. Her experience shows us that we may be living and experiencing layered dimensional time. When an incident happened in this time exactly as it was happening in a previous time, her and her friend's energy from this dimension seemed to unite with their energy from another dimension bringing the two dimensions together that would have normally only been a Deja Vu effect. Since they were reenacting the same experience of death the souls were somehow brought together, because when the souls leave these places of dimensional time they are returning to their full consciousness that is waiting in what we call heaven, a place not bound by time, but is eternal. I know that sounds way out there, but there's more. To top that off they were different genders in these different dimensions which means, when we are sent back to these areas of time, living in physical bodies we can return as any gender, any race, any religion and any nationality. I do not have to tell you what that implies, other than we are truly more the same than different. We are spiritual beings that were given the gift of living a physical life. If I were to ask myself why? It is all too clear. The Creator has already shown me that he completely controls the power of matter & energy. He can instantly change either one. There is no God vs. Science, He is what we call science. The only possible reason he would do all this would be for us to learn from these earthly experiences so that at some point they will no longer be needed and the old souls that learn what is important will be the final souls that will live eternally with the Creator. Those future living beings will have learned enough to have become like minded with the Creator. I know how this sounds, but remember we are only putting the pieces together. As for religions, they are a moral compass for mankind, helping us to be morally good, but life itself provides all the tests we need to pass for an eternal future. We were never handed the whole story, just enough to keep us in line. When you read the bible, it is filled with irony, so the fact that God might send a white supremacist back to be a black slave, makes perfect sense if the outcome was to make you a better soul. Men who rape or hurt woman would probably come back as a woman. The soul must experience all sides to learn and understand. Now you're thinking then why we don't remember these previous lives while we're here. For the same reason Jesus did not know about his life in heaven until the Holy Spirit came upon him. It would be counterproductive if you were already predisposed to believe a certain way. This would make it impossible for you to learn something new. I believe just as our consciousness can separate to live in different times, our full consciousness remains with God until all our energy comes together in heaven and the realization of what we have learned is kept always with our full consciousness no matter where our soul may be. The bible also refers to God as being outside of time for he already knows the past and future. When we finally get to live eternally there will be no need for our consciousness or the lives, we've lived to be kept separate, our soul will remain complete. Since God already knows the outcome, this whole learning exercise is so that we will know and get to where He already knows where we will be. None of this is important for you to dwell on now. Keep with your religion and most importantly always have a good heart, for it's the condition of your heart or your intentions that will always bring you back to heaven, as we can't buy our way into heaven not even with good deeds, but it is through good deeds that our intentions are known.

I believe animals also are filled with an energy or spirit and that they also are a part of the spirit world, but their spirit is not a human soul, just as a human soul is not a part of the angelic realm, but because of the little bird the day of my husband's funeral, I feel our energy can exist alongside of theirs. I'm still connecting dots as I promised. People that did bad things while they were alive, like the gang member I talked about, seemed to have been sent to a place of deprivation, total darkness, no sound, and unable to talk or communicate. It's not known how long he would be subjected to this, before getting another chance or even if he would get another chance, but I do believe that God loves all of us, even the worst of us. The only thing that I feel he will not abide is evil or evil intention. Therefore, I don't believe an evil soul comes back or will ever get a chance for the ultimate state of existence which is eternal life. The real meaning of Hell is being cut off from the Creator, for He is the source of all things and all life.

Now it would be comforting if my life experiences would leave us in the knowledge that our Creator allows spiritual beings to live a physical human existence experiencing the physical lineage or DNA that comes within each ripple of time. If only I could stop there, but I have been allowed to interact with a variety of phenomena. As we connect the dots, we know God has kept us, within his care. However, there are other beings in other galaxies that also have physical bodies, we do not know the extent of God's relationships with those creations, but we know they exist. I would even go as far to say, some of their visits made them want to be able to blend in with us. Whether they could complete that task is unknown, but after my experience with them I was very drawn to that artwork that showed children with exceptionally large eyes. I even bought some of the artwork, but the weird thing was I never hung it up on the walls.

I've been interacting and co-existing throughout my life with the spiritual world. In most cases they are souls for whatever reason haven't moved on yet. I feel at times this may be a good thing, as the spiritual realm that surrounds us isn't always a good energy.

There are energies that do not mean us well and at times these good souls that haven't left yet help us, but there are forces that even they can't handle and that is why we must always stay close to our God in faith. These dark forces have pushed their way into my life, and I let them know I belong to God. God has never forsaken me, nor will he forsake any of his children and his power is greater than all things as He controls the universal energy and all physical matter. God's holy active force that came to me, wants me to share with you the knowledge that he is always with you. Build your relationship with God, by talking to him, he is listening to you, he loves you. Being in his presence makes you realize no matter how much you love your family, your friends, and your love of life itself, in the end He is the only thing that matters. He will dry your tears and he will hold you in the palm of his hand. He loves you so much, because he created you, not only physically, but right down to the last spark of energy that makes you who you are. You can think of this power as God or you can think of it as the universal power of all things, it is the same.

I have written other books, but this book I am writing is to please, God. I know I will most likely receive terrible criticism, along with the ignorance of hatred. Understanding it makes no difference to me if you want to believe these things or not. I'm not fighting to keep your soul close to God, He is fighting for you to want a relationship with him and all I am doing is trying to please him. Having said that, I truly do wish you well and I pray for your success and happiness. Do not turn away from God, you need him, and he loves you.

People will say, *"What makes her so special?"* The answer is I'm Not, but the people reading this are and collectively we are the special everything in God's sight, we've been searching always for his presence that has always been with us. The religious history of the Jewish people has provided basic principles that you can find in all Christian religions, but to be truthful God sent out his truth in many ways to all humanity.

Then the moral compass began, where we were all in search of our own truth. Keeping the basics from old, we branched out into many denominations. God had given righteous understandings among all the lands unto all the people. This never changed righteousness for there is right and wrong, we understand these principles. I say unto everyone, it doesn't matter what religion you are, from East to West, North to South. All the Prophets that walked this world, spoke to all of us. Jesus was never a religion; he was a way of understanding sent from God for all of us to emulate. He came and died for the world. He was the walking breathing testament of God, our Creator, our Father in Heaven. Jesus Christ was a doorway of truth, a window into the goodness of heaven, and he in no way discounted or undermined all the other Prophets and Saints that came before him or after. God's love has always been upon all of us, He is with you Now, and loves you dearly. He will not invade your life, but if you speak to him, he will listen, if you ask of him, he will answer by helping you according to his Will. There is one more reason for this book, it is to prepare you, for there will be others that He will come to and I'm sure there will be other messages for all of us. Have no doubts that you are not alone, even before you were born God was with you.

ANGEL'S MESSAGE

I had a miracle happen Aug. 2018, that I had documented it in real time on my twitter account. I had a dream where I saw a pool of crystal-clear water in front of me. One drop of my blood fell into the water & the water remained clear. I called my daughter & she said that she also had a dream that same night. A hooded being, came to my daughter that she seemed to know in another place or time which I will call an angel came to her, He called her by name then said, *o tell my 27 yr. old* I froze when she said that, because I had a scratchy throat for a long time & I wonder if that could be a sign of cancer, but I just ignored it. I didn't believe that anything could be wrong because I thought it was just postnasal drip from my allergies and I had had several checkups. I posted this on twitter & went to the doctor the next day. Lots of tests were run & the doctor didn't think it was anything, but she did two final test & one required surgery. The pathology report came back that revealed I had cancer & they thought it was two types of cancer. I said to the doctor who had been saying it was probably not cancer, *"I guess the angel was right."* She hugged me & I went in for the complete removal of my thyroid. I feel as if God sent me to this doctor and I felt very good about the surgery that I had on Nov. 30th, 2018. I was then told that I would need radiation to clear up any remaining tissue. The day came for my radiation and I went to tell my 27 yr. old granddaughter who was staying with me at the time that I was going for my radiation treatment. She sat up in the bed and said that I could not have the radiation treatment. She explained that she had been dreaming and God interrupted her dream to tell her that if I went for my treatment today that I would be dead before she woke up. I went anyway to see what the doctor would say. My son in law had taken me for my treatment. When the doctor came in, I asked him if he thought that I should have this treatment. Now understand that I had plenty of insurance, the appointment had been set way ahead of time and I have never had a hospital turn away money. The doctor acted very strange as he replied, *"Well you can have it or not have it, it is really up to you."* My son in law and I looked at each other and I said, *"well if it is not that important then I am not going to have it."* and we left.

I went back to my primary doctor and he was terribly upset that I did not have the radiation. He said that because I did not have it that any remaining cancer could have traveled to another part of my body and now, they would have to find out where it went. So, my doctor ordered blood tests, and everything came back cancer free.

My daughter and granddaughter have filled my life with mountains of joy and happiness. They both have such a beautiful spirit that is kind, forever giving and they both had a dream that saved my life. I love all my family and I pray that they will be blessed, for they have all been a blessing to me.

I'm hoping at some point I will be opening a *"God's Visit Foundation"* to help with cancer research, cancer patients, plus donating to help the homeless & stray animals which are causes close to my heart. God Bless us all, remembering miracles are all around us all the time.

"There's as many atoms in a single molecule of your DNA as there are stars in the typical galaxy. We are, each of us, a little universe."

— Neil deGrasse Tyson, Cosmos, never forget that you are amazing.

AUTHOR'S THOUGHTS

As you have read this book you have felt my pain and known my thoughts. My thinking has evolved through my many different experiences. When I was young it felt like walking on water through Hell. There was an unseen force that was always there with me. We all have access to this force. It comes from within, reaches out, and connects with the power of the unseen spiritual world. It is surrounding us all the time. A form of energy that is an awesome power. Tapping into it is like tapping into a main power source that engulfs the universe. I believe that it is what we call creation, the infinite power of intelligence. We were meant to tap into it, but sometimes we are pulled into it by a governing power or intention. One thing for sure it is connected to us physically & spiritually.

Death is neither the end nor beginning, we are in a constant state of existence. The only difference is the form. We are either in the state of energy or matter and we travel between these two states of existence in the constant mode of learning. We not only learn for our own spiritual awareness, but everything we experience good or bad, God our Creator is experiencing it too. We are that connected to him. That is why many times when we are in our deepest moment of despair he reaches out into this world and helps us. The only thing that can stop him from helping us is our own will of defiance. If we've chosen not to believe in him, we have in essence shut that connection down.

He lets us take a part of our consciousness into this world, keeping the greater part of us with him, as it would be unproductive to try to live a new experience when we would already be filled with so many. We are truly spiritual beings that have chosen or been given the chance to live a physical life. We come into this world with physical characteristics and traits from our present physical being's lineage, but we also have inner spiritual traits. We see what is going on in this world, but the world we came from is all around us and I think at times even rooting for us when they see what we are going through. Our essence or energy returns to the power source from which it came, hopefully more evolved than when it left the spiritual world. The power source of the universe is an entity within itself that has no barriers like dimensions or time. Therefore, it is the basic governing power of all living and spiritual existence. No one can escape the judgment of this power, nor do we ultimately want to. I believe the whole journey of life is to learn, enjoy, and gain approval from this power. If we can feed upon this power during our life, it will bring happiness and a sense of peace, but when we turn from this power it has a starvation effect of agony, fear, and the pain of life becomes tormenting. The soul needs nourishment just as the body.

There is a truth; there is a temple. The temple is you; the religion is the discipline of hearing and acting upon the word. The word of truth is what makes the temple strong. When the world is judged, I believe the ones that shall be saved will not come from just one perfect religion. They will be saved if they are the temple of truth. How will you know the truth? The truth will respect all life, it will be selfless, giving, forgiving, caring, understanding, sharing with the less fortunate without regret or expecting something in return, it will be self-sacrificing, it will have patience, it will be hopeful, it will be kind, it won't lie to you, it will be honest, it won't speak ill of others, it will never be greedy or envious, it won't hurt or cause pain, it will encompass all that love stands for and you will feel it's goodness in your soul. If you make a mistake you will always come back to what you know in your heart is right.

Who are these people of this truth? They are the people who reached out to you when you needed help. They are the people who picked you up when you fell-down. They brushed off your feet and put your shoes back on. They are the people even in their own hour of need reached out to help others. It isn't a deed that will save, but a true love for goodness, a faith in a greater power than one's self, a belief that a great sacrifice overshadows us all regardless of our faith. Not all religions will feed the truth. Only a pure heart will be able to discern the truth, as the veil will be lifted from their eyes. The intuitive soul will know, the body will feel, and the heart will confirm.

Everything in life needs balance and right now everything is out of balance in our world, it is spinning out of control. You can't control this world or the universe, but you can try to maintain self-balance as much as possible. You know that every action has a reaction, so keep things positive in your heart and mind. This will cause what is positive in the world to be the reactions that you will face. When you have a pure heart, it shines like a light and people are naturally drawn to it.

A perfect example would be Reverend Joel, some people put him down because of the favor that he has received in his life. Make no mistake it is not about money even though his ministry has been blessed and he is not the only light that shines brightly for I have met others like Reverend Temple, Reverend Richard and there are many more. When they speak, they light up the darkest night just as easily as they would light up a cathedral. They would speak the same words with the same love, whether they were in a church, on a campus, or in some ditch anywhere in the world. When we genuinely want to be a servant of the most-high God, there is no hiding the light that people will be drawn to. When they come, and they will, just be the precious person God made you to be. There will also be evil come your way and people who hold darkness in their hearts. When they come pray with them, share your love for God, but if they continue to mock you walk away and find higher ground for you need Not to be approved and accepted by no one. You were approved by God long before you came into this world and there is no greater love or approval in the entire universe than His. Remember you are not alone and when you feel like you are carrying the whole world on your shoulders reach out and ask God for help. For He is always with you, like a Father with his toddler that is trying to walk for the first time, he waits to see if you will need him and the moment you do he will pick you up with the biggest smile, because he knew that you were trying to get it right all by yourself. Now I can tell you that in the short time that I spent in God's presence I had a chance to realize many things. You are going to have a hard time with what I am about to share, but I really need to share it with you, especially with what the world will be facing. We separate God and Science, with our constant God vs. science. God Is science. I don't know how to make it any clearer. God is the universal energy and can change energy into matter and matter into energy, I've seen this, but cannot expect you to believe. He can hold our energy close to him or allow it universal freedom. Since he can create matter, he chose to make beautiful worlds for us to experience, enjoy, and learn about the true nature of goodness vs. the true nature of evil. He not only created our world, but he also created a way for us to learn. He layered time and our soul or consciousness can return into these layers, causing us to experience similar events many times throughout our lives which we refer to as DeJa'Vu. I believe that this layered time starts from the beginning of mankind and ends upon what the bible calls the first resurrection where we live a thousand years. The reason I believe it stops there, as the second resurrection will be all the souls, that understand the true nature of God's goodness and from that point on those souls will have earned the gift of eternal life. Understand I am a mere messenger, as we all are when we share our experiences, I am not a Saint, just an everyday sinner trying to do what is right. I had a dream about humanity's future, but I do not consider myself a prophet, like you I must pray for my miracles, but they have entered my life many times over. The best part of being the messenger is that you only need to deliver the message and it is up to those who receive it, to take it into their heart or throw it away. That is the most wonderful part about you and me, that we have lived through many of the same hardships, we have rejoiced over many of the same blessings, and even with all these things I have shared with you, we are more alike than different. If I could give you one gift that in the end would be greater than all gifts, it would be the gift to believe. Do not let anyone take that away from you. They shall truly try to tell you that you do not know what you are talking about. They will constantly throw it in your face to prove it but remember their mouth and their so-called wisdom cannot disprove what your heart knows to be true. In the end, you will be eternal, and they will be No More.

I hope you will enjoy the many Tweets I placed in the back of my book and I hope it will give you some insight into my heart, mind, and soul. I've been trying to put the pieces together to make sense of my life, but I'm aware that I may not have all the pieces of life's puzzle. I more than welcome hearing from my readers if they know something that would help me to understand things a little bit better. If you believe in nothing else in life, please believe that you were created to be eternal and the only one who can change that is you. I pray that your dreams will come true and that your life will be filled with blessings and favor, and may God bless you & your family always, Amen Never forget that God is with You and that He loves you very much.

Remember God Is the Creator not People.

There is a Pro-Life movement, but it is not about life.

For if it were these same people would not do everything, they can to do away with all the programs to help children and their families.

The Truth is only God chooses who is given the gift of life.

John 1:13 Which were born, not of blood, nor of the will of flesh, nor of the will of man, but of God.

No Republican can make a child to be born & No Democrat can stop it, ONLY GOD.

Don't be fooled by all the Hate & Corruption, it's not about abortions or how many weapons you can own. It is about Caring for all Humanity and the Unity of mankind.

God is with us, He hears our every Word

I was driving to work one morning feeling very sad about the fact my Grandson was always filled with so much anger. He is disabled and has swelling of the brain which at times causes his moods to become unbearable to deal with. I started praying asking God to cast out the Hate & Anger that seemed to control his life. I told God that I was fearful of the person that he had become and tears flowed down my face. For I was his last hope as No one wanted to deal with him and his disability. I told God to send me a sign that if he had healed my Grandson that my Grandson would say to me out of nowhere, *"Granma I'm Healthy."* I came home that day and took him as usual to the store and when we came home he said something to me as he was getting out of the car, but I couldn't quite hear it. I rolled the window down, as I was collecting my things to get out of the car and said to him, What did you say? He walked over to the window and repeated his words, *"Granma I'm Healthy."* Remember always God will not forsake any soul.

Rainbow Road

My 35-year-old Grandson and I were on our way to the grocery store. It had just rained and the ground was covered in water. We were traveling west down 38th Avenue in St. Petersburgh, Florida and we looked to our left and saw this beautiful Rainbow coming down from the sky above actually touching the ground. My Grandson immediately said, Grandma where is the pot of gold? I was shocked because I thought, it was impossible to see where a Rainbow touches the ground. I noticed people were driving through the Rainbow and said to my Grandson let's turn around so that we can drive through the Rainbow. I quickly turned around into that lane traveling east, but to our surprise coming from the other side, you could no longer see the Rainbow.

We looked all around us, but from that side, it was not visible at all. Then for some reason, a significant truth came into my mind. Sometimes the truth is there, but even if we are completely surrounded by the truth we can't see it, because we are going the wrong way! This completely summed up our present political environment, of how people are completely blinded to the Truth, because they are going the wrong way!!!

Meteor Shower

A young man said to me I had this spectacular dream last night. I dreamt there was this magnificent Meteor shower. I could Not take my eyes off it as I was in awe of its beauty. Then I woke up. Several months later a young woman came to me saying. I had this incredible dream last night. It was so real that I could even smell the air. I was standing outside and I saw this Meteor Shower coming into the atmosphere. I looked up to my left into the night sky and saw ships from other worlds, as if they came to watch the spectacle. Then I looked up into the Heaven's and saw a Fireball hanging up in the sky with a space then another Fireball, then a space then another Fireball. I instantly realized these Fireballs were being controlled by those on Earth and they were about to be released into the atmosphere along with the Meteor Shower. Just before the Fireballs were to be released, I looked straight up into Heaven and I saw God, Jesus, and the Angels appear. The world ends with this!

You Are Being Tested

The world right now will be facing a challenging time. My work will not change that, but it will help all the people who read it to face the challenges that will come upon them. People believed that Trump-et was meant to show them the way, but he was only meant to divide the world, causing great havoc, pain, and discontent. I wish this would not be so, but when he was elected the 1st time and the 6th trumpet sounded over Israel to show that he was the one that would make way for the greatest deceiver of all times. John the Baptist indeed made way for Truth, Love, & Unity. John the 6th Trump-et will now make way for Hate, Lies, & Division. Throughout my life, I have experienced the impossible, along with people from all walks of life coming to me with unusual stories. I wish I could tell you things are about to get better, but I'm sorry to say they are about to become extremely difficult. I want you to remember you are not alone on this journey called life and believe with all your heart there is a power of great love that is right there with you. I am sorry for what you are now facing, God Bless you & may you see the Truth! After you read it pass it on, for it will be like a torch in the darkness for others to see their way. I received a letter from President Joe Biden, he did make some mistakes, but he believed in freedom for all people, as my forefathers believed before they came to America.

This is a Warning for all humanity that make it to the End of our present time. Israel will have built their last Temple and the Anti-Christ will have been at the Temple for 42 Months before the End. The Red Heifers will be ready for Sacrifice.

I must warn you, do Not stand against this being for No One will survive coming against him. Deep down inside you will know to flee and run away from this Evil for you will Not survive it.

When this feeling comes over you no matter what you have or don't have, no matter where you are "Flee."

For God the Creator of all things will provide for you and all those that are with you no matter where you run, but you must Not stay for this wicked power will consume all that comes against it.

May the God of the Universe be with you remembering that we are Spiritual Beings living a physical life.

I Love you all God Bless you Forever.

"DIVINE GUARDIAN"
BY SANDY OLSON

Is a fictional story inspired by the many unusual events that happened in my life, including some of my real dreams & premonitions, only the dreams & premonitions from the book "The End Is Our Beginning" can only be considered truthful.

"Angels in the Night" by SK Stevens" (Sandy Olson)

Is a song that seemed to come to me out of nowhere, it is sweet & calming, with Tampa Bay's best drummer three years in a row. I told him to make the drums roll like thunder and he did.

Web Page
sandraolson0912.com

Good Morning World, you have now entered into a time of Great Division, Hatred, & Deception! There is Nothing you could have done to stop what is coming for it has been coming for a long time. It was the only way that Creation could ultimately separate those who are deserving & ready for a beautiful New World. Only those with a good heart will truly embrace Love, Truth, & Unity and will walk through into this New World of Hope. The hearts filled with Hate, Lies, & Division will be lost forever in Darkness. I am sorry for what you are now facing, God Bless you & may you see the Truth! I explain many of these things in my book "The End Is Our Beginning" by SK Olson

The heart of the United States of America started beating in England, Europe, & the entire world hundreds of years ago. We have a rare opportunity to awaken the hearts of all Humanity that truly believe in a better life for everyone and a future that will guide their existence into a New World of hope. Please don't let this moment be lost in History. Our only chance to open the eyes of all Americans may very well be right now, helping us to remember where we came from and the Dreams that brought us to America. That is why I will be sharing with you Birth certificates of my ancestors who came here to start a new life. As part of my Web Page I'm sharing with you pieces of my life. I've enclosed parts of my youth like being a Cadet in the Civil Air Patrol & being a part of the Masonic Order as a Rainbow girl, my Mother was an Eastern Star. My life started out dying then being brought back to life at 5-Years old. I was taken away from my family living for a period of time with Rev. Stiers his wife Brenda & their 2-daughters Heather & Gretchen. My Web Page is filled with all the little moments &

broken pieces of my life. As a Teen I worked for the Southern New England Telephone Company. When I was in my early 20's I started working for TRW Geometric Tool, a tooling division that was highly technical & working on significant Space Programs. For a short time, I attended Grace Downs Air Career School only to return shortly back to TRW Geometric Tool. My life was an Education through on hands experiences, not an education through schooling. I opened my own Subway Franchise, then I went back to working on NASA projects at Honeywell & General Components. I also became an inspector for Transitions Optical & became a Realtor for 10-Years. All the pieces of my life on this Web Page are like snowflakes floating & changing. A life filled with unusual happenings dancing between the beautiful soft shapes of snow flakes & at times turning into burning ashes that fell upon the earth then out of those ashes rising like a Phoenix soaring between reality & the unknown. Fly with me back to a world of Love, Truth & Unity. May the Angels always be with us.

TWEETS:

"As we grow older our path becomes covered in what we have learned, & what we have experienced, towards the end of life our path is covered completely in the fallen leaves of understanding."

"The whole universe blooms with the same energy, through the light & love of our Creator."

"I'm going to hug the trees, inhale the sweet fragrance of the flowers, squish my toes in the soft grass & cool sand, feel the soft breeze upon my face, listen to the babbling brooks, peacefully float in the ocean, love the animals, protect planet Earth."

"It is the people who can't see with their heart, they can't see with their soul, they can't see past the obvious & clearly can't see past their nose, they are the people that someday will be awakened into the world we already know."

"God is a power that can rock the universe, or He can wipe away every tear in your life. I Promise."

"There is no darkness that we cannot overcome, for the light is in us & the energy of the universe is with us for we are loved."

"You can have faith in a greater power, knowing that this eternal power wants what is best for you & loves you without religion. Religions are a moral compass to guide us, to a greater understanding, real faith comes from within, it is not given, it is a part of your soul."

"Jesus came into this world to validate all that was good, including all the good prophets of righteousness, to deliver people from religious burdens that were placed upon them, and there is no one on this planet that He would leave behind."

"I look upon the glimmering light that passes through my world; Knowing it has brightly passed through the spirit world; It brings me joy to see this light twinkling in my world; Knowing that it need not change a sparkle passing world to world" Sandy O.

"The true beauty & wonder of the unknown is knowing that we are a part of it."

"The path to everlasting life is always narrow, for it is not for those who think that they alone know the truth and are content to leave behind all those who see things differently. God loves all of humanity, don't forget to love him."

"When you need a new perspective don't be afraid to be a little bit different. We are all programmed with what should be instead of what could be."

"Memories are the reflections of our life that we take with us when we leave this world."

"When your path stretches out into the unknown, God will help you to find your way to having a good life, for you are never truly alone."

"No matter how many mountains you climb you are not alone, for God is always with you."

"God will always place a song in your heart & He will always filter light into your life to help you find your way."

"Even when your heart hits the ground it will still beat with love, it will still care for family, and Almighty God will still feel & know the goodness your heart generates for your soul."

"Sometimes your dream isn't even meant for you, but you dream it anyway for the sake of others."

"No words are needed for love and kindness, for you can feel love and you respond to kindness."

"When your best friend needs a hug, they can count on you to care."

"To know God is to know that whatever is His will is to be rejoiced even in pain, for He loves you and has not dismissed your suffering. God will always filter light into your life to help you find your way."

"Within a single molecule of your DNA, there are as many atoms as in a typical galaxy, and why not we were created by the very hand of the universe."

"Everyone then who hears these words of mine & does them will be like a wise man who built his house on the rock. & the rain fell, & the floods came, & the winds blew & beat on that house, but it did not fall, because it had been founded on the rock." Matt 7:24-27

"When your life flows over a cliff, don't worry just float down the river with hope in your heart and favor will begin to flow with you."

"Our earth is alive, and it constantly lets us feel its pain and anger, as I watch a volcano erupt it looks like blood flowing from mother earth. Let us respect this planet Earth for it is a gift."

"Balance life with peace & harmony, then you will live happily……. Ever After."

"Sometimes we need someone that doesn't mind helping us to get to where we are going." "Some flowers seem to burst forth in celebration, for everything is intentional through God's love, his holy grace, and favor & we are a part of it."

"To have pets brings an incredibly special joy into your life." "Just like the peacock, walk with dignity and when you rise high in life fly with grace."

"I walked across a field at night, I came upon a tree of fright, A blood red sky all around, The moon glowed upon the ground, Shadows floated behind the mist, Murmuring softly, make a wish, I said, let us all be blessed & safe, A doorway opened to a future place"

"Love knows No difference in being, it only listens to your heart." "Love and goodness are universal truths that contain all that we will ever need, everything that opposes it is deception and lies."

"Our journey never ends, it just crosses over, for we're only visiting this physical realm to feel, understand, & learn. If we don't lose our light in the darkness, we will live forever with the eternal beings that have always been."

"Hold onto your dreams even if they seem to be melting away, for when the time is right, they will emerge with beautiful wings and take flight all around you."

"The mystical magic of this universe comes from an energy that lives within all of us and lights our way. Listen to your heart, cross your bridges, and know that you are loved."

"When an animal finds their person, it will just fall asleep in that person's loving arms."

"I have walked away most of my life because I felt there was still hope for someone to change, but I shall never walk away knowing someone else will be victimized. I can choose to be a victim, but I will not choose to be a Coward!!!"

"The more you hurt others the lower you will fall; A good heart keeps rising through & above it all."

"The tree of life sparkling within the universal garden, constantly growing with energy that comes from deserving souls of goodness that will live forever with eternal beings that have always been."

"When your friend knows that you could use a little kindness, they help you get past your fear of getting into the deep water."

"Even if you are the only flower in the grass you were meant to be there, for it takes each of us to make this world beautiful."

"Love and kindness are the only things that matter, for in the end you will receive mercy according to your kindness and judged by the goodness of your heart."

"Sometimes what we need most of all, is what we already have, don't forget to recognize your blessings."

"The greatest love is when you care more for someone than you fear for yourself."

"We are, what we are, and what we could be within the seasons of time, except for our spiritual being of energy, for that part of us has been blessed to be a part of eternity. Be earthly angels of kindness."

"God knows your heart and hears your every word, speak to Him for He is there for you."

"The innocent can see things far more clearly, for they have not been fully programmed by our worldly system and they have not been filled with a lot of preconceived thoughts & notions. They can see the true beauty in everything."

"Architecture always seems to speak to the time that it was created in, Notre Dame De Paris, and speaks with passion and love, architecture in our time has hard lines for society has become cold and indifferent towards life."

"Our body stays grounded reaching out to the world above, then one day our soul will fly towards the heavens and dance among the stars."

"There are many beautiful wonders in this world, don't forget to remember that you are one of the many wonders, you are unique, and no one shines quite like you."

"You may feel like your life is flowing over the rapids but hold on and soon you will be flowing into rivers of opportunities and blessings."

"All flowers bring beauty into our world, for it takes every flower to create a beautiful garden. It takes every person to create a beautiful world."

"Evil is the absence of God; therefore, God is the cause of enlightenment & evil is the effect without that enlightenment. Now don't confuse this with good & bad for they are just two sides of the same coin." "When you can talk to someone who loves what you love, your time together is always like a symphony."

"When you can dance upon the wind, you have a good heart and a soul that sparkles with energy."

"God is intelligent energy, our true self is energy, our home is a world of energy, & all the physical matter in the universe comes from energy. Reality is only a perception of what we feel must be our truth. So, make your dream your own reality."

"Humanity is a beautiful wonder of creation, our physical being encases the magic of our soul that was created to be eternal."

"The Celtic culture believes that angels plant daisies to bring people joy. Your Creator knows every tear that you have ever shed in your lifetime, and one day when you return to Him, he will gently wipe them all away. I promise."

"Friendships are blessings meant to protect your heart from sadness."

"To be a soul is infinite, a spark of energy traveling the speed of light, but to be a soul within a physical body upon a beautiful planet is a gift, to be able to understand how precious existence is when you now face the delicate fate of mortality."

"When you feel like your whole world is out on a limb, and you still feel safe, it is because you realize that there is way more to your existence than this physical world. You have never been alone, and you are loved

"Sometimes the purpose of our life is in the journey itself, be grateful for the blessing of just being alive for it is a gift to help us to understand."

"A good friend is a treasure that we find in our hearts." "I looked unto the heavens and it appeared as if it were an ocean of gold, and I realized the treasures that we possess. The curtain of the day is a mere illusion, as the curtain lifts the truth becomes clear we're a small planet in a vast universe that sparkles with hope."

"As I watched the whales, I realized that the gentle giants of the sea, are so graceful as they glide through the water."

"There are times when the past seems to still be alive walking forever in the present among those always in the future."

"Friendship gives and sometimes friendship takes away, but in the end, friendships are worth it all."

"There are doorways that we can clearly see, and there are doorways that only our spirit can open, but sometimes we pass hidden doorways in life and where they go is a mystery, like walking down a path that seems to disappear right before our eyes."

"We look upon the same moon, we see the stars sparkling in the heavens, we are one humanity, let's never forget that."

"Sometimes in life, you cannot tell up from down, when that happens stand still for a moment and let God guide you through."

"I've crawled through life like a caterpillar, now dear God let me fly like a butterfly."

"Many military people come home to a world that they fought for but now feel invisible. We need to do better as a country for those who have sacrificed for us."

"Learning is seeing things from all sides, otherwise, it is not learning it is staying with the same perspective that you were already programmed with, a picture is never truly clear until you see even what you choose not to. Perspective can be everything."

"When the sun visits Earth, it becomes a sunflower, always following its true self in space, enjoying the soft rain & cool breezes that it can never know within its truest form. When the sun is not out the sunflowers face each other and share their energy."

"Art is like a butterfly, it crawls through a creation process unnoticed, then suddenly its inner beauty emerges causing it to flow through the hearts & souls of humanity."

"We can fly like the eagle if we keep hope in our hearts and listen to the goodness in our souls, for righteousness lifts us up and helps make all our dreams come true. May God's blessings be upon you & his favor be with you always."

"They can chain your body, but no one can chain your soul."

"At the end of this world, as we know it our last moments here on earth will blend together with all our colorful attitudes, we will be all the *love we've known, & we will shine like the brightest moments of our lives. For our end is the doorway to a new beginning for all of us."*

"There are times in life when we are laden down with burdens, so frozen & unable to take care of everything, but never give up hope for the one constant in life is change."

"We all should agree that we are not here to focus on the negative, we are here to live a good life and to bring the positive into this world."

"Peace is our calm, Anger out the Storm, and God is our only

Hope."

"When your life is a straight climb up the side of a mountain & you just can't hold on, let God know you can't go any further and He will send you a ladder to make your climb easier. For He hears you and He will help you."

"When you stare into the eyes of nature, the universe stares back at you."

"When we are with God, we know only love, when we first come to earth it is still a part of us, until the world tries to strip it away."

"Sometimes comfort is just one heart beating next to another heart."

"There is no greater gift than a true friend, for they do not look to judge you, they only try to understand your side of everything & be there when you need them even in your silence."

"As the autumn leaves flow down around you in a poetic peace, bringing you a multitude of blessings upon your journey, know that God has a plan for all of us, you need only to reach out to Him."

"As life carries you down the river & over the falls make every moment count, don't judge your life by what you did or didn't do. If each moment mattered, then you did what you came here to do. You are unique & you are loved."

"Life is a dance, let the music fill your heart and touch your soul with joy."

"When I look at the Banyan tree it symbolizes eternal life due to its seemingly unending expansion. The branches extend towards the heavens & reach for the earth much like us, our physical body holds onto the earth & our spiritual energy reaches for the stars."

"Our lives flow with passion, we take flight with love, and we are understood through the gift of friendship, Joy is all around us don't let it slip away."

"Like the flowers in the field, our time is precious and lets us live our lives caring about each other, sharing an abundance of kindness before the last petal falls."

"Butterflies are unaware of how much joy they bring into our lives, just like the innocent they have that same delicate beauty that is so very precious."

"Sometimes it is so extremely hard to let go, but once you do it will be so easy to move forward. Not everyone's journey in life goes in the same direction or takes the same path, we are all here to learn."

"I find the most comforting thing about the day ending is that there is a peacefulness to the night's sky, knowing we are not alone and that the morning is always a new beginning. Have a beautiful day."

"Cross your bridges with hope in your heart for you never know what opportunities may come your way on the other side, be courageous for you are never truly alone in this life."

"And so, the owl is right, we do not love, we only fight, life is short & will be gone, having missed our shining dawn, free your heart & let it Love, peace will come with pure white doves, listen please humanity, for the sake of you & me."

"God sent us many Saintly Prophets to help guide our steps and they all preached goodness, kindness, and a love for all mankind."

"May the glorious light of love & kindness always be upon us." "Life is filled with raging storms, that fill our lives with fear; This too shall pass, as we know God's hand is truly near."

"They knew things back in the ancient days that even to this day we still do not comprehend."

"The end of our path isn't always visible, but if you keep hope in your heart & believe that there is an indestructible power watching over you, then all that you need to finish your journey will be provided unto you."

"We are spiritual beings living a physical life, we are only visitors to this planet, for we were invited through birth, but we come from a world of energy."

"Sometimes our world blends together, it's as if there is no time, no direction, just every moment reflecting the last, keep hope in your heart & your life will change when the moment is right & you will find yourself in what feels like a whole new life."

"A friend will dance with you when there is no music, they will sit with you when you don't want to talk, they will listen when you need to be heard, they will not judge you, they will help you if you let them, they will never abandon you."

"When earth reflects the heavens & our heart reflects our soul, then life is as it should be, "heaven on earth."

"Nature's Cathedrals are blessed with light that pours down from the heavens, places of peace, places of divine grace."

"Children always have that look of wonderment & depth in their eyes, for the very young still see with their souls, and not with a mind that has been programmed by the world."

"The moon is our planet's companion, its force is felt upon the earth, an eternal friendship that touches our earth with light and energy, a connection that we can easily be a part of."

"Trump-et is so much like the golden calf, the man who comes down from his golden tower, to offer the masses a sense of power, but just like the golden calf that has no heart, he will only lead them into serving his needs and providing their destruction."

"Don't let your life be the reflection of others, break free to see things clearly with your own heart & soul, or you will blend in with all the other trees of what you have been programmed to believe."

"The world has turned its back on life; Every day is filled with fear & strife; A trail of thickened blood quickly flows; when will the answers come, no one knows; thoughts keep turning round & around; We can't seem to quiet the roaring sound"

"Earthly angels are a blessing we should treasure, for their hearts beat for those in need."

"When life seems to split in half right before your very eyes, remember things are not always as they seem. Hold onto your dreams for they will become your reality."

"God will always give you strength & He will filter light into your life to help you find your way through the storm, all you must do is believe in a power that is greater than all things."

"When planet Earth starts erupting all we can do is step aside, for we are merely visitors to this world."

"Let's give planet Earth the respect that she so truly deserves, and not destroy her beauty."

"Every moment in life is like a delicate petal, each moment falls away quickly, but when you stop and look back you can see the beautiful garden of your life."

"Be especially kind on your bad days, for the good energy that you put out will turn your day around & it will become one of your better days."

"The power of God can rock the universe, or He can wipe away every tear in your life."

"There are as many atoms in a single molecule of your DNA as there are stars in the typical galaxy. We are, each of us, a little universe."

− Neil deGrasse Tyson, Cosmos, never forget that you are amazing.

"Just like the leaning Tower of Pisa, we were made perfect, but we tilt a little when it comes to living life."

"When the peace of a dove touches the heart of a hawk, he becomes the power of an eagle."

"Never doubt your own self-worth, as the energy of your spirit & physical being was created by intelligent design, you are part of a greater picture, you are more than this life, and you have a purpose."

"When you know inside that you can fly, but you just need a little help. Sometimes blessings come when someone else recognizes your dream and helps you to fly." "

Every stepping stone in life was meant to help you make your dreams come true, you are incredibly loved, and you will never be forgotten."

"As our soul stands in the vastness of an infinite universe, it is a part of the universal existence, creation's physical experience through life. Our Creator loves us & never forgets where we are. He will always help us find our way home."

"Energy flows into our world for we are connected to an infinite power source & we are more than this life. You are never alone & will never be forgotten."

"It is imagination that dictates our future, for we have the power to pull that universal energy of desire into our world. Dream big and may your dreams come from a place of goodness that will benefit all humanity."

"When the curtain of day lifts the truth becomes clear, we are a small planet in a vast universe that sparkles with hope."

"If we could see the steps that we have climbed in our life, the steps may not be stacked so neatly, but sometimes it isn't always how we made it, the blessing is in arriving."

"Our lives, our oceans of learning & understanding, and what you keep within your heart & soul will determine which side you have chosen & your ultimate dwelling for eternity. The Atlantic Ocean will not mix with the Pacific Ocean, just as Good & Evil do not mix."

"God will always surround us with hope, beauty, love, & an entire rainbow of understanding."

"Sometimes you need to stop struggling against the weight of the wave & allow the wave to pick you up & carry you to a better place. God allows tragedy to help you move forward."

"As you look back upon your life, you will see a life covered in blessings."

"God is with us, He hears our every word, He knows the intentions of every heart, and He will not forsake any soul.".

www.ingramcontent.com/pod-product-compliance
Lightning Source LLC
Chambersburg PA
CBHW051212120626
46547CB00013B/1321